Zen ^and_the Art ^of Intimacy

The Simple Path of Passion,
Fidelity and Love

Arthur Samuels, M.D.

Element
An Imprint of HarperCollins*Publishers*
77-85 Fulham Palace Road,
Hammersmith, London W6 8JB

The Element website address is: www.element.com

and *Element* are trademarks of
HarperCollins*Publishers* Ltd

Published by Element 2004

1 3 5 7 9 10 8 6 4 2

© Arthur Samuels 2004

A catalogue record of this book is
available from the British Library

ISBN 0 00 717688 0

Printed and bound in the USA

DEDICATION

To all my ancestors who made me what I am today. To the Creator who provided soul food for their work. To my wife, Kari, who keeps teaching me the meaning of enthusiasm ("in God"). To my children, Shepherd, a guardian of music and law, and Marianne, whose joyful and loving spirit transcends death. To Christian Allman, her husband, who loved her as no man before has ever loved a woman and who valiantly put the pieces of this book together in a last-minute editing. To Daniel, his wife Nona, and my grandchildren, Leah and Vera, who are the guardians and essence of family love. To Erin, my youngest daughter, who keeps growing in wisdom and her capacity to love. To my editor, Gregory Brandenburgh, who suggested this topic to me in the first place and had the faith in me to convince his colleagues that it should be published. To my patients who courageously joined me in a quest for intimacy. To Bob and Mary Goulding who made the psychology of people more understandable. To my two great Buddhist mentors, Thich Nhat Hanh and Reb Anderson, whose wisdom continually infuses me with the light that never dies. And finally, to my readers, who had the patience to go through this book. Thank you all from the bottom of my heart for validating my existence.

CONTENTS

INTRODUCTION

Alan Shore, a neuroscientist at UCLA, has shown that in infancy, the normal development of our brain depends upon the quality of parenting we receive. The implications are obvious: **We are hard-wired to be close to others**. It is a basic need, virtually as essential to our health as food and water.

Many other studies have shown that those of us who are in supportive relationships live longer and healthier lives. Even our genetic structure is influenced by mutual caring. The foundation of our basic morality comes from how close we were with our parents. Bonding in a mutually supportive, loving relationship with one another and with God is essential to our well-being, the health of our families and the positive development of our civilization. This book is dedicated to overcoming obstacles to bonding. You can start right now with a smile of appreciation from your heart to someone you want to be close to.

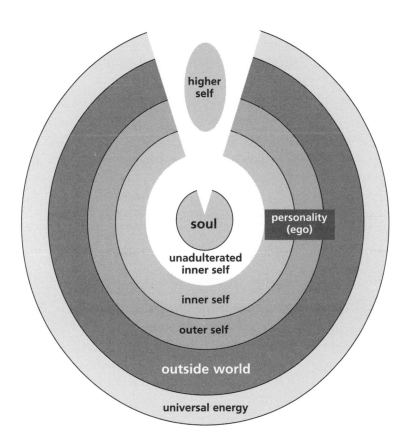

higher
self

soul

personality
(ego)

unadulterated
inner self

inner self

outer self

outside world

universal energy

TABLE A	TABLE B
Qualities Present in the Core Self *(Soul, God Within, Buddha Self, Universal Energy)*	*Characteristics of the Inner/Outer Self* *(Ego)*
Compassionate	Judgmental
Loving	Fearful
Wise	Opinionated
Receptive	Intrusive
Allowing	Dominating
Unlimited	Limited
Intuitive	Rationalizing
Sense of oneness with other people	Seeks fixed position
Sense of inner strength	Clinging
Total aliveness	Controlled
Mindful	Restrictive/reactive
Spontaneous	Conventional
Creative	Anxious
Inspired	Defensive
Peaceful	Separated
Open	Identity seeking
Connected	Stresses differences
Touches present Reality	Nature ignored
Oneness with Nature	
Outer Softness	
Evolving	
Humble	

*Section I: Zen and the Art of
Intimacy with Your True Self*

PRELUDE TO
INTIMACY

A TREASURED MEMORY FROM
A DISTANT PAST

A hot day in Germany
War winding down
Alone with a rifle guarding a bombed-out railroad station
She alone too
Walking down a dusty road carrying shoes
She comes closer when I call her
The shoes are for orphans in the next town
I'm touched by her mission
And melt when she offers me food
She who has so little to offer
I give her water
I kiss her parched lips
They too are giving
I brush away the broken glass
And take off my tunic
We lie together on the stone floor softened by caring
Body and mind torn by war
Healed by the love of a stranger
I shall always love
But never saw again.

As I compare that treasured moment from my distant past with the richness of marriage many decades later, I am filled with a sense of wondrous gratitude and joy. In a world of accelerating impermanence and danger, my love for my wife and her love for me serves as a haven and a repeated source of joyful resurrection. It is a springboard for a moment-to-moment romance with life. Like that brief interlude in my nineteenth year of life, long-term love pierces the darkness of uncertainty. Yes, intimacy is possible in a brief encounter, but this book is designed to help you discover that the delicious sharing of the body, mind, and soul we call "intimacy" can be infinitely more satisfying in the committed long-term relationship.

The information garnered here represents the culmination of a lifelong personal quest. More importantly, it is the fruit of the combined labors of hundreds of wonderful people I have worked with in the past forty years – strangers joined in a common search for intimacy.

For most of us, the journey to closeness is marred by storms or boredom. My heartfelt wish is that *Zen and the Art of Intimacy* will enable you to be the love in the center of any storm that comes your way, and help you to reach that priceless treasure – love that lasts forever.

In this book you will learn to experience commitment not as restrictive or limiting, but as a protective bond in which you and your partner can flourish. You will learn how to transform anxiety and depression into a sense of peace and wellbeing. You will also be empowered to change anger into patience and compassion, and convert longing for idealized romance into real and gratifying caring. Most importantly, you will discover the joy of unconditional love for yourself and your partner, unfettered by past experiences.

WHAT DOES ZEN HAVE TO DO WITH INTIMACY?

What does Zen have to do with intimacy? Everything! Zen is a form of meditation, a practice that enables you to be totally in this moment – the only moment in which you can ever live. In practice, Zen opens the way for loving feelings to emerge naturally from deep inside you. There is no need for grabbing or controlling, no waiting for something in the future or clinging to the past. It confirms your individuality as a lover as well as your connectedness to your beloved. You are interdependent, co-arising in harmony with all things in the universe.

Zen masters have developed practices for many centuries that facilitate a state of mind conducive to unadulterated love. Each chapter that follows represents an integrated application of modern psychological techniques with the wisdom of both ancient and modern-day Zen masters. My gratitude is heartfelt and deep to all of these teachers.

Zen meditation, in a very real sense, is almost synonymous with intimacy. When your life partner is the object of your meditation, you are touching them with the fullness of your mind, free of intervening thoughts. You are not judging or labeling them in any way. You are not controlling or backing away. The silence between you is imbued with loving awareness or your interdependent connectedness.

WHAT IS ZEN?

Zen comes from a major school of Buddhism. Since the fifth century BC, it has been used as a means of making the practitioner meticulously aware of moment-to-moment thoughts, physical sensations, and emotions.

Instead of reacting to our thoughts or physical sensations automatically, as we usually do, the meditator learns how to let them pass and feel an inner tranquility. With practice, the meditation experience provides a wonderful sense of enlightenment – a state of deep awareness of a connection to all things in the universe and oneness with the Creator. It is very similar to meditations used by Christian mystics to experience what is called "Christ consciousness."

I have adapted this approach to lead us to identify how reacting mindlessly to thoughts alienates us from ourselves and distances us from the person to whom we want to be close. The technique achieves this on a moment-to-moment basis. Rehearsing this process, as this book will teach you to do, will open you up to experiencing the marvelous intimacy that is beyond words.

THE NEUROBIOLOGY OF MEDITATION

Scientists are beginning to discover the neurobiology of different meditative states. For instance, at the University of Wisconsin, an advanced meditator was asked to focus on compassion, a major component of love. When he did this, there was a marked shift in brain-wave activity to the left, prefrontal side of the brain, a center for feelings of happiness and other positive emotions. Untrained volunteers who were also asked to focus on compassion showed prefrontal activity almost equally divided between the right – a locus of negative emotions – and the left sides.

Where the activity is in the brain has a major effect on the emotions felt. This study and others give strong credence to the effectiveness of meditation. I have used these techniques with almost all of my patients for the past ten years. The vast majority have succeeded in learning how to use meditation to prevent or quieten negative emotions, or transform them to positive ones. Stop for a moment and imagine what this can do for your love life!

Still, the psychoanalyst in me says, "That takes care of the present. How about the root causes of painful emotions that occurred in childhood that are still bubbling up in the present?" That's a good question. The answer and healing for old psychological bruises that still hurt are found in other meditations and exercises in this book. These are adapted from modern psychological disciplines such as transactional analysis, Gestalt therapy, hypnotherapy, and existential psychoanalysis. But don't let all of these arcane topics discourage you. The actual practices are easy to understand, simple to follow, and effective. They provide almost immediate relief. Practiced frequently over time, the changes made are permanent. As a result, you will find it much easier to love yourself and your mate unconditionally.

IS THIS BOOK FOR YOU?

✤ Have you ever tried to be close to someone, only to find the harder you tried, the more distant he or she became?
✤ Have you ever ran from someone because they seemed interested?
✤ Have you ever had a relationship seemingly inexplicably fall apart?
✤ Have you ever feared you will never be able to have an intimate relationship?
✤ Is it scary to commit yourself to one person?
✤ Do you feel lonely and long to be close to someone?
✤ Do you find yourself angry, sad, or anxious much of the time with your intimate other?
✤ Has boredom dimmed the sparkle in your marriage or long-term relationship?
✤ Have you started looking for love elsewhere?
✤ Are you thinking of splitting up?

If the answer to any of these questions is "yes", you will be delighted with the solutions in *Zen and the Art of Intimacy*.

Your Love is Here to Stay

You may have lost some slenderness, some innocence, some hair, even some of your health since those golden days when you first met that person who was to become your long-term lover, husband or wife. But the one thing you can never lose is your capacity to love. You are about to learn how to rejuvenate that love.

Sharing the ups and downs of life with one person over a long period of time brings with it a sense of stability. In a world of ever-accelerating change, it provides a home base to feel safe in. Building a good life together is the perfect antidote to alienation and loneliness. When children are involved, it provides crucial underpinning for their sense of inner security, a safety net that stays with them the rest of their life.

The book you have in your hand at this moment will tell you how to maintain a long-term relationship. The exciting part is that you will be able to do this without suffering the tedium that often comes with familiarity. The lyrics of the old song go "The Rockies may crumble, Gibraltar may tumble, they're only made of clay – but our love is here to stay." This book is dedicated to making that dream come true.

A Long Gestation

For forty years I've perched on the edge of emotion, wanting to shout obvious directions to couples who longed for closeness. I soon learned that even helpful advice was demeaning to their problem-solving capabilities, and quickly forgotten. On the other hand, compassionate understanding and shared solutions brought tears of relief and happy hugs that gave life meaning.

This book is the cumulative result of hundreds of strangers bonded together in their search for love. It identifies and provides solutions to the major obstacles we all must confront as we seek a healthy, intimate relationship.

What this Book Can Do for You

We will be addressing and finding solutions to the major problems we all must confront in seeking a healthy, intimate relationship. With its practical, easy-to-follow exercises and case studies, *Zen and the Art of Intimacy* will help you to:

- ❖ Experience commitment not as restrictive, but as a protective bond in which you and your partner can flourish.
- ❖ Overcome both conscious and subtle fears of intimacy that may be out of your conscious awareness.
- ❖ Transform anxiety and depression into peace.
- ❖ Fill your inner void without searching for fulfillment outside of the home.
- ❖ Change anger into patience and compassion.
- ❖ Convert longing for idealized romance to authentic love.
- ❖ Turn the boredom of familiarity into an incubator for exciting growth together.
- ❖ Transform the longing and anxiety of the "roving eye" syndrome into positive energy by learning how to extract what is most attractive about a third party and incorporating those traits into your own personality and your current relationship.

- ✤ Go through the "seven year itch" without scratching.
- ✤ Find inner beauty when outer beauty fades.
- ✤ Discover how to achieve and maintain true intimacy by giving up attachments to either negative or positive emotions and judgments.
- ✤ Become a soul mate with your partner.

How to Use this Book

Do you love yourself at this moment without reservation? Do you accept your present limitations without criticism? Can you enjoy inspiring yourself to change and grow? These are the goals of the first section of this book. The more you are able to love yourself unconditionally, the easier it becomes to do the same for someone else. Differences between you open life's horizons rather than clouding them with conflict. The second section of this book will help you overcome the burdens that keep you from maintaining the magic of staying in love in a long-term relationship.

In your search for a lover you had to browse about before you found someone who caught your eye. Then you needed time and patience to develop a real relationship. Use this book in the same way. In perusing the table of contents, you will find some of the chapters particularly intriguing and go directly to them. But taking the time to really familiarize yourself with all the chapters sequentially, and to repeat the exercises as much as is necessary, will be well worth your while. The more intimate you become with the book, the more intimate you will be able to become with your true self and the love of your life.

YOU ARE
MORE THAN
YOU THINK
– GETTING TO
KNOW YOU

We relate to our lover with only a small part of who we are. Look at the chart on page XI and notice the diminutive area labeled "ego" or "personality" and you'll see what I mean. Actually, all of that circle is us – our potential to love and be loved is as vast as the universe itself. In this chapter and the next, you will discover how we restrict ourselves – and, even more importantly, how we can free ourselves to be more than we think.

We start by taking a look at our inner and outer selves that form our ego and our personality. Our personality is the cloak we put on to present to the outside world. I will describe how our egos and personalities are formed and constrict us. Then we will identify and use the unadulterated higher parts of our selves to reverse the process of constriction and learn how to give ourselves permission to experience the higher levels of ourselves and the full majesty that is truly us. Our capacity to love and be loved is limitless.

THE INNER SELF

This is most likely the part of us we think about when we refer to "me." It is the part that feels guilty when a police officer stops us although we may be innocent of any wrongdoing. It is the part of us that groans when the alarm clock goes off in the morning. It sparkles when someone smiles at us or when we enjoy some lively music. It feels expansive when it is loved and contracts defensively when it is criticized or hurt.

The voice of the inner self says things like "I'm sad," or "I'm angry," or "I feel great." At other times, we suppress its voice. When you feel physically tense or are suffering pain in your body that doesn't come from an injury or illness, that pain represents a muffled cry for help from the inner self you have locked tightly inside your body. This part of you is the heir to your childhood. When strong stimuli hit you, they activate memory traces of when you were a child. At those times, your inner self may consist almost entirely of thoughts, feelings, and physical sensations identical to those you had as a child. For example, if your boss or spouse is angry at you now, it might ignite memory traces of your dad yelling at you when you were very young. Your self-perception might shrink in size and you may feel exactly as you did at that early age. Your inner self can range in age from infancy to your present age – i.e., it could be your inner child, your inner adolescent, or your inner adult.

The Inner Child

As an infant, our inner self is totally congruent. We express exactly what we want, both physically and emotionally. On the chart on page XI, notice the inner self's proximity to the soul self. Small children are much more in touch with the joy of discovery and creativity than adults. This wide-eyed openness and curiosity are at the heart of our spiritual wonderment of the mysteries of life.

Unfortunately, layer upon layer covers what was originally a spontaneous, authentic part of us. This occurs because the inner self adapts to the expectations of parents and society. Some of these adaptations are necessary for survival. It is necessary to adapt in order to become a part of the culture we are raised in. If we were respected and loved as young people, our inner self retains much of its basic integrity as it learns to adapt. We are more likely to maintain a true contact with our spiritual core because being nurtured in a loving way makes us free to love others unconditionally, as if they were an integral part of ourselves.

If our upbringing was harsh or if we were punished or discounted for having our own opinions, or were mistreated just because we expressed our own needs, we had to learn how to discount and ignore what is vital to our being. Many of our body sensations may become foreign to us. Severe physical tensions, which ordinarily serve as a red light telling us to stop and take care of ourselves, are ignored. Our inner self in many ways was replaced by images or roles more acceptable to our family and our culture.

Your inner self may be unaccustomed to being cared for by you. In fact, it may distrust you and stay at a distance. That's what is going on when you feel tense, angry, sad, or anxious – "out of sorts" or "just not with it." In a few moments, you will learn how to take care of that.

THE OUTER SELF

This is the part of us that interacts with the outside world. It is the part that controls and molds the inner self. It was formed in large part when we were children. Imagine yourself as a sensitive, wide-eyed little person experiencing the world around you. Using these observations, we construct an outer self, or an internal parent, that sets rules for the inner self to follow – a tactic designed to help us best survive the childhood world.

Constructing an Outer Self in a Harsh Environment

In a harsh and unloving environment, our outer self sets strict rules that ignore the best qualities of our inner self. Our true loves and authentic needs are throttled in order to adapt to the spoken and unspoken expectations of our parents and other authority figures in our environment. At worst, trying to survive this problematic world, the outer self we produce betrays the essential loving and trusting nature of the inner self. We become blind even to its basic physical requirements. For instance, if you are exhausted but force yourself to continue working, the outer self is saying, "I don't care how tired you are. You have got to get this work done. Do it well, or I'll punish you with disapproval."

We may not be consciously aware of what we are doing. In fact, we have often trained ourselves to barely feel the tension and fatigue. We can't hear the cry from the inner self because we are prone to cover these feelings up by doing what the outside world says we should be doing. The messages say, "Stay cool. Ignore the tiredness. Nobody wants to hear about it. Don't complain. Be strong. The bad feelings will go away. Have a cup of coffee and liven up!" But the inner self still feels bad and it signals its discomfort with depression, irritation, even physical breakdown.

As the outer self loses contact with our basic humanness, it does the same with the humanity of other people. It becomes more critical rather than loving. It looks for faults in others rather than being supportive. It concerns itself with manipulating others rather than being with them. It limits us to following rituals and political dogma rather than searching for true meaning. It cannot see the outside world clearly because it takes a mental picture of the conflict going on in your inner world, projects it onto the outside and then reacts to it as if it were real.

And for us, it is real. For example, if we are constantly pushing ourselves to be productive, despite our physical or emotional state, everyone and everything around us is seen as demanding, although they might not be. In fact, to conform to our "pushy" childhood rules, if the people around us aren't pushy enough, we might quit and seek a more demanding job, or divorce our spouse to find a more "ambitious" one. The opposite is true if our outer self is egocentrically indulgent of our inner self. In that case, we might expect the outside world to indulge us and become furious when it does not.

As the needs and talents of our inner self are obscured and distorted, we feel afraid, sad, or angry. We long for peace – the peace that comes from total acceptance of the inner self. Instead of feeling compassion, the outer self is often critical of these emotions in its quest to meet the demands of the outside world. When this occurs, we feel bound down and unfulfilled no matter how hard we work. We long for "freedom."

Constructing an Outer Self in
a Nurturing Environment

If, on the other hand, we are raised in a nurturing environment, the part that becomes our outer self sees that it is safe to keep what is uniquely "us." The controls are loving ones and are as responsive to the needs and growing interest of the inner self as they are to meeting the requirements of the outer world. We then feel free to be ourselves rather than live up to some unreasonable or unrealistic image. In those conditions, we grow up loving ourselves and engage in work with a sense of creative freedom. It is also easier to love others unconditionally. We don't have to search the world waiting sadly for someone to come along and love us to fill our inner void because there is no inner void – intimacy with others is easy and fulfilling precisely because we have learned how to be intimate with ourselves.

PERSONALITY AND EGO

The personality we use to face the world reflects this conflict between the inner and outer selves. Sometimes it is colorful, showy, and extroverted. Sometimes it is subdued, drab, and introverted. It represents the outer costume the ego wears to present to the outside world. It might be a critical and harsh carbon copy of our own parents or a withdrawn and timid extension of our frightened inner self. It could also be the opposite of our parents' personalities. In rebellion, we could develop the personality of an anarchist and may become totally indifferent to all rules. Raised in a loving, secure environment with rules that are truly designed for our wellbeing, the personality we develop and present to the outside world will be a responsible one, because we care about people and ourselves, but also permeated with a charm that uniquely expresses our free inner self.

You Can Change Your Personality

Perhaps the greatest addiction is to our own personality. We tend to become more and more locked in the prison of behaviors that fit our particular way of presenting ourselves to the outside world. Acting in a different manner makes us feel very uncomfortable.

As you will discover, once you learn how to love and accept yourself as you are, without judgment, you will feel peaceful inside. Then you can explore many different ways of encountering the outside world – ways that will be in harmony with how you feel. **Then you will be able to explore many new personality traits, keeping the ones that enhance your life while discarding those that impede it.** You may even decide that you love the way you have always been and keep that same personality. That's fine – as long as it is a free choice.

SOUL

The soul self is your unadulterated inner self. It has different names in different religions. It might be called the Christ or Buddha or Allah self – but whatever it is called, it is made up of universal, or God, energy. We are born with it and it is unchangeable and eternal. It is there before our birth and will be there after we die. Rabbi Joshua Liebermann once said, "We are all little pieces of God." Our soul self is our own very special piece of the Almighty, the anointed one, the universe.

If you are not a follower of "organized religion," you might be more comfortable thinking of this divine part of yourself as a fluctuating, harmonic energy field. It is in total and complete harmony with the vast central energy field of the universe. It is a portion of time and space – the mystery core of scientific inquiry. It is what all things are made of and it is nothing at the same time. One way of understanding this concept is to look into an electron microscope and see where matter turns to energy and energy turns into matter. When you are in your soul self, you are engulfed in an aura of peaceful love and generative excitement that can best be labeled as blissful.

The soul self is represented in the chart as your very center (see page XI). It is the bull's eye that, when you touch it, offers you all the wonderful experiences listed in Table A (see page XII). It automatically connects you with your higher self and God self (universal energy). The exercises you will be learning will help you access this wonderful part of you.

Table B describes how we usually are as we operate out of our ego – shifting to Table A is a journey to nirvana!

GOD SELF OR UNIVERSAL ENERGY

This is the same material as the soul self. It is found everywhere – in all things and in all people. "God is not a person, but not less than a person. God is the ground of being," wrote the theological philosopher Paul Tillich. God self is the inevitable, miraculous energy with which all things are created. Since everything stems from it, we all have this bond in common. All people and all things are indeed children of the Creator. Knowing and feeling this produces natural love for the world around you and everything in it. After all, everything that has been created is your kin, part of your family. This is the ultimate energy you tap into when the different parts of your personality and your mind come to a quiet place.

THE HIGHER SELF

In the diagram notice the pie slices labeled the "higher self" (see page XI). This is connected to all other parts of you. It is the center of mindful wisdom for both the inner and outer self. It is deeply connected with your individual soul self and with universal energy, or God. Because it remains uncontaminated, it actually comprises your only unobstructed, undistorted, non-judgmental view of yourself and the outside world. It is mindful, deeply compassionate, loving, and understanding. It is the part of you that watches your thoughts when you meditate and gives you the sense of being profoundly loved and accepted as you are.

The higher self functions like a magnificent computer that scans all parts of you, dips down into your soul self and comes up with the answers you learn to recognize as true. It provides you with the wisdom you need to sail through the ups and downs of everyday life.

NOW FOR SOME ACTION!

We have been talking about what is. Now let's walk our talk and discover what can be. In a few minutes, you will actually feel what it is like to move out of that cave of unhappy feeling into the sunshine of peaceful, fulfilling thought and emotion.

The Inner Self Meditation that follows works like magic. It changes that critical voice in your head into a loving one. You become your own healer or therapist. It helps heal painful childhood memories buried in the body as it transforms unwanted emotions in the present. It changes you from a grump into a lover and clears the path for deeper meditations – communion with the Creator within you.

INNER SELF MEDITATION

No matter how old we are, there is a tender childlike part inside of us – a part that longs to be accepted and loved. That part of us may range in age from newborn to our present age. The inner self, as we've learned, seeks love and nurturing when in pain and enthusiastic support for achievement. Ordinarily, that part of ourselves looks outside to lovers, friends, and relatives for this kind of approval. But if good parenting wasn't available in childhood, the need for it from outside becomes that much more critical.

Meditating on the inner self provides perfect parenting – the kind most of us never had. Once you learn how to do it, you will be able to take care of uncomfortable or counter-productive emotions rapidly. You'll become less dependent on your partner, husband, or wife. You will have less need to seek approval from others.

Giving yourself unconditional acceptance and love makes it much easier to give it to your partner. It's a simple procedure that works – and the more you do it, the more effective it becomes. Use it many times a day, especially when you feel sad, angry, scared, or confused. But it may be even more important when you are feeling good. Cheering yourself on for having good feelings will become a wonderful new habit.

Meditating on the inner self occurs in seven steps. With practice, you will find it works like a miracle cure for painful emotions. And it takes only a few minutes each time you practice:

INNER SELF MEDITATION

Step 1 – Identifying Your Emotions

Emotions are simply labels used to describe thoughts and physical feelings that occur in your body. *For example, when your muscles contract and your heart beats faster, you might call this anger – or you might call it fear. If you are tired, listless, moving around slowly, you might call this depression. It is important to learn how to identify minimal levels of emotions because they can grow into an avalanche of feelings that overwhelms your clear thinking. Start by simply watching your thoughts or your physical reactions, letting your mind rest on your breathing. Watch your breath and tell yourself, "I'm breathing in; I'm breathing out." As you focus on your breathing, you'll notice thoughts intruding. Watch the thoughts and determine the predominant emotion associated with your thought patterns. Do you feel calm, excited, sad, scared, or angry? Just label it.*

Step 2 – Thought and Physical Sensation

A positive emotion may be experienced as a rush of energy. An unwanted feeling is contained as tension somewhere in your body. Slowly move your mind's eye over your body from your toes to the top of your head. Where in your body is the feeling most concentrated?

Step 3 – How Old You Feel Inside that Emotion

Ask yourself: "How old do I feel inside that emotion?" and visualize or sense an image of yourself located in that part of the body where the emotion is centered. The expression on the face of that image is probably the same one you are feeling now. You might just have a vague sense of your inner self there or the picture may be very clear. You may see yourself as an infant, child, adolsescent or your current age. Which age shows up for you right now?

Step 4 – Activate Love and Embrace Your Inner Self

If the image is that of an infant or small child, imagine taking them onto your lap and holding them tenderly and lovingly. If it is an older child or adult, put your arm caringly around their shoulders now. There is an important switch here in your emotions. *Recall a time when you felt very caring – open up to that loving energy now and breathe it in. The love may have been for God, a person, a pet, or even a plant. Let it grow with each in-breath and send it to your inner self with each out-breath. If you have difficulty feeling love, recall a time when someone was particularly loving to you or to someone else. Imagine being that caring person. Feel the soft gleam in your eyes, the warmth radiating through your body. Imagine you are not imagining. You are that person, full of compassion and understanding and permeated with a flow of loving energy that you now send to your inner self.*

Step 5 – Accept the Emotions

Breathe in the emotions your inner self is having now. Feel compassion if the emotion is a painful one, or excitement if it's a positive one. You are holding the inner self and letting the emotions come to you, accepting them completely and fully, with deep caring. The compassion, you will find, completely burns up the negative emotion; you might imagine it going up in smoke. As you breathe out, you send your inner self love and caring.

It is important to remain very patient and mindful, staying completely focused on your inner self. You are, in effect, giving it the total attention it never received, except perhaps in early infancy. Be aware that patience is the traditional antidote for anger and is also the basis for love. In fact, patience and compassion are the essential foundation of love. More than anything else, this precious part of you needs unconditional love and attention. When your mind starts wandering, very gently bring it back to the child. In this process of total acceptance, you are not criticizing or evaluating the emotions.

Be careful not to discount what your inner self experiences with platitudes such as, "It's alright, you'll feel better soon." You are deeply understanding and accepting that your inner self is in pain and that you are there completely for it. If the emotion is a positive one, you are there to rejoice and reinforce it.

Compassion means feeling passionately with someone else, putting yourself in their shoes and feeling their feelings. Sending compassion towards the child is love in action. Let yourself feel the joy of being the comforter. Loving pleasure overwhelms pain and transforms it.

WHEN YOUR INNER SELF DOESN'T RESPOND
Your inner self may be used to looking elsewhere for love, and it may distrust you if you have been self-critical. You might even sense your inner self standing at a distance, distrusting you.

Continue to be patient and compassionate. Accept the distrust as you breathe in and send it love as you breathe out.

Don't expect the inner self to respond right away. Don't expect change and certainly don't push for it. If you do this, you will be just like the parent who may have caused the damage in the first place. The perfect parent you are now accepts and loves the inner self as it is, and lets change occur at a natural pace. As you feel your love for the child, it helps to physically smile. At first, it is a tender smile of compassion. Welcome in tranquility as it occurs and smile with joy that the inner self has become more comfortable with you. Exhale your pleasure that it is feeling better. Soon, you may see the child smiling back. Feel your excitement and joy as you respond to the child's smile.

Step 6 – Connect with Universal Energy
At this point, let yourself feel the exquisite sense of grace that comes with loving yourself, not because you had to do something to earn it, but simply because you are alive.

You are a part of God's universe. As you breathe in, feel yourself drawing energy from out in the universe, feeling yourself one with all creativity and the Creator. And as you breathe out, feel the grace and wonder of being part of it all, with the beauty and majesty of life itself.

Step 7 – Resolve the Issue
Now, feeling the calm inside, take care of whatever it was that disturbed you in the first place – some loss or conflict between the inner and outer selves. Take care of it now or make some concrete

plan to take care of it in the future. In this way, you are not only taking care of the inner self on the emotional level, but also on a practical level.

CASE VIGNETTE

M arty, a graduate student, was so anxious at exam times that he was unable to focus enough to pass. His tension was focused in his throat as he visualized himself to be a young teenager.

His teenager inner self resented the long hours of study imposed by his harsh, perfectionist outer self and passively resisted studying by daydreaming about dating.

As Marty practiced the Inner Self Meditation, he could clearly identify his internal struggle. He learned to replace criticism with compassion for his teenaged self. His solution was to take more time out to enjoy dating – the study time lost was more than made up for by being able to concentrate when he did study. With repetition of the Inner Self Meditation, and resolving the conflict, he was able to retain the information he studied and lost his fear of exams.

The underlying existential conflict for Marty was based on the realistic fear that his perfectionism made unrealistic expectations that would leave him with no time or energy for love.

Summary of the Inner Self Meditation

1 Identify your current emotion.

2 Locate where in your body you feel the emotion.

3 Picture an image of your inner self inside that place, expressing your emotion.

4 Activate a loving feeling and embrace your inner self.

5 Breathe in the emotion with compassion if it is painful or joy if it is positive. Send loving energy to your inner self with each out-breath.

6 Connect with universal energy.

7 Take care of the precipitating problem at a practical level or reinforce the positive experience by doing more of it.

HOW WE BECOME CHAINED BY OUR OWN THOUGHTS

Our thoughts and emotions limit us to living in our little self or our ego. These thoughts and emotions have remained fundamentally unchanged in their basic messages about ourselves since childhood. Stop for a moment and check this out for yourself. What is your favorite bad feeling now? Sadness, anxiety, anger? Chances are that same emotion permeated your thinking when you were a child.

Who Am I?

Thoughts produce a physical reaction. We label thoughts as neutral, sad, angry, or happy. We then call that sequence of events "me." Since most of our thoughts today are the same as those we had yesterday and will have tomorrow, "me" (our ego and personality) stay the same. Since nothing in life is permanent, trying to hold on to an inflexible identity produces tension and bad feelings. It makes it very difficult to be flexible and stay in a good intimate relationship because we defend our ego as if our life depended upon it.

Our concept of our self is based on who we *imagine* ourselves to be. Actually, we are more like a kaleidoscopic image in a constant state of flux that varies with everything going on in the universe. We are not independent, fixed things. As Buddha described it, we are in a state of dependent co-arising, and everything around us is in a state of dependent co-arising with us. If we free ourselves of the thoughts we bind ourselves with, we can always be a fresh breeze to ourselves and others. We do that by moving into our higher self.

How to Break the Chains with a Feather

Instead of reacting to our own thoughts like a dog chasing its tail, we can step out of that conditioning/reactive cycle by moving into our higher self. From the higher self, which is a diffuse form of love without words, we embrace each thought, emotion, or physical tension with loving awareness and mindfulness. Touching the thought with mindfulness is like a magic wand that penetrates through superficial meaning into a wider and deeper experience.

Here's how to move into the higher self. Eventually you will be able to move there easily simply by reminding yourself of its existence and letting yourself go there. Until then, meditating on your breath will lead you there.

MEDITATING ON YOUR BREATH

❖ *Sit upright, neither leaning forward into the future or back into the past where you are attaching yourself to old thoughts and emotions.*

❖ *Shift your focus away from the thoughts in your head to your abdomen, lowering your breathing to your abdomen.*

❖ *Watch your belly rise as you breathe in and fall as you breathe out. Be mindful of the nature of each breath. Is it shallow and tense or smooth and relaxed? Think the words, "I'm breathing in" with each inhalation, and "I'm breathing out" with each exhalation.*

❖ *Now, focus energy on the out-breath, particularly the quiet space at the end of the exhalation. You continue breathing in and out and are more and more focused on the end of the exhalation.*

❖ *Don't try to stop your thoughts. Notice them as if they were birds flying by and return to your breathing.*

❖ *You will notice the flow of words slowing down as you move your attention more and more into the quiet space.*

✤ *You are now into your higher self. From that place, be mindful of your thoughts.*

✤ *Let the deeper meaning and wisdom from the higher parts of your mind seep in like a whisper or a dream. Try this with the word "love."*

You can use this same meditation to focus on an emotion or a physical sensation. It softens the boundaries of the experience and fills your being with love and wisdom. This is intimacy with your true self. When it touches the true self of your lover, it is literally heavenly.

In Chapter 3, you will learn how to identify and change outmoded rules for living. These rules confine us to being a character acting out a prescribed script, a story we created for ourselves as children in an attempt to best adapt to our family of origin. Free of that script, you will be able to create a new life with the one you love.

I WANT TO
BE FREE

W e're on the way to freedom – let's keep charging ahead. The last chapter showed us how to exonerate ourselves from our own thoughts and emotions. This one does the same thing on a broader scale – our whole life story. It is fascinating to become aware of the script we create for ourselves as children, and exciting to change that to moment-to-moment living free of that story line. This frees us to be flexible enough to be lovingly present in the ups and downs of intimacy with others.

ORIGIN OF YOUR LIFE SCRIPT

D o you feel bound down by things you have to do, people you have to please or take care of? Are you tying yourself up in knots attempting to be perfect or do your best? Do you feel as if you can't really start living until you make some major changes in your life? For example: *After I get that new job, or when I graduate, or after I move – then I'll be able to enjoy life*.

If your answer to any of these questions is yes, you are probably caught in a role you created for yourself many years ago. This chapter explains how you may have trapped yourself into a restrictive life pattern or "script" as a small child in order to get the love and approval of those who raised you. Even if you rebelled against your parental figures, you created for yourself a personality that can be, at best, very limiting. You may be outgoing, shy, or withdrawn. You might pour yourself into the creative mold of an artist, or that of a hard-working business person. You may even thrive on behaving as a criminal. Or you may be scripted to become a good mother or father, or a responsible citizen, or you may be an irresponsible thrill-seeker.

Whether the role you have cast for yourself happens to bring success or failure in our culture makes little difference as far as the sense of feeling free inside is concerned.

You fall in love with the people who help you either fulfill or break free from these expectations. In due time, you feel trapped by your own self-image and you may experience the same fear, sadness, or anger that was familiar to you as a child. The trap of self-expectations feels suffocating because you are not experiencing your full potential – you are, in fact, limiting your own options for the very freedom you crave.

Being unaware that you are inflicting this painful situation on yourself, you might blame your partner. Feeling uncomfortable at home, you might seek "freedom" by having an affair or getting a divorce. But you are taking your trapped self with you – your pain is compounded because you have alienated yourself from your family.

Bound Down by a Script We Write for Ourselves

I can offer several examples from my own psychiatric practice as well as my personal life. As I approached middle age, I had a successful career that I had worked hard to achieve and a family I loved deeply. But I was miserable much of the time. I felt completely tied down by the life I had created for myself. Subconsciously at first, and more overtly over time, I began to harbor an intense need for freedom. Still, I didn't really know what I wanted to be free of – I only knew I would be depressed until I experienced that elusive sense of freedom I sought. I had trapped myself into a life script and my sentence was to live it out.

All of us do that to some extent. Even if we rebel against who we are supposed to be it doesn't really help. Being locked into rebellion is a painful mockery of freedom.

The unwritten manuscript that determines much of our personality, and how we will live our lives, is decided by us – when we were children. It is built around the genetic material we are born with. The story line, for the most part, is shaped and restricted by unspoken and spoken rules and guidelines set by our parents and the culture in which we were raised.

To begin our journey to freedom, it is helpful to identify some of the rules we consciously or unconsciously follow in creating our life role. Once we are familiar with them, we can choose to let go of those that don't contribute to our well-being and explore the unlimited potentials with which we were gifted at birth. Being intimate with (mindful of) who we are frees us to become who we can be.

NEGATIVE RULES FOR LIFE*

The legacy many people create for themselves may include a long list of injunctions – or negative rules – that were either overtly expressed or unconsciously mandated

---

* Following up the work of Dr Eric Berne, Dr Robert Goulding and his wife, Mary Goulding, identified these rules and employed them in Redecision Therapy.

by their parents through their behavior and the way they treated them. Some children follow these rules; some do not. But the influence of these injunctions plays a major role in the formation of your personality. Their effect on the course of your life continues, unless you learn to recognize them and change them.

Some of the rules include:

Don't Be: A child is beaten physically or emotionally injured when in their parents' presence, or the parents might simply ignore the child entirely. This potentially malignant message may be spoken or unspoken. In any event, it is saying, "You have no right to be here, or no right to live at all." Almost all suicidal patients have received this injunction. This is the most malignant injunction of all. It is also prevalent in people who repeatedly and recklessly risk their lives through thoughtless self-destructive behavior or taking in food or chemicals that are toxic to their health. The unconscious decision is: *I'll be an obedient child. I won't bother you with my existence. I'll have an accident or kill myself.*

Don't Be You: Parents may have repeatedly told the child in one way or another that there is something wrong with them and they won't be loved until they become how their parents expect them to be. This could include admonitions to be smarter, thinner, sweeter, tougher, sexier (or less sexy), taller, prettier, cunning, loving, or any other injunction that fails to accept the child as they are. This injunction produces a life-long fear of expressing or even having one's own emotions and opinions. It leads to a feeling of not being acceptable to yourself or to other people. You have a strong fear of rejection.

Don't Be a Child: Very early in life, a child may be chastised for being too loud, boisterous, or unruly. The message is that the child should be more serious, more like an adult. To have fun is considered childlike, silly, and unacceptable. This injunction results in an aversion to being spontaneous and enjoying yourself. You always keep your nose to the grindstone of reasonableness.

Don't Grow Up: These messages can be enhanced by overprotective parents. They are saying, "You are really incapable of doing that." The unspoken message is that you are not mature enough to take care of yourself. *Stay a child so we can feel safe in our important roles as Your Parents.* As an adult, you feel afraid of being responsible and become dependent on others to take care of you.

Don't Be Successful: Parents who communicate this message are habitually critical and fail to support their child's efforts to achieve. A parent's sense of adequacy may in fact be threatened by their child's talent, intelligence, superior education, or attractiveness. This can also stem from overprotectiveness. *You'll get hurt if you stand out in any way.* You may grow up knowing that you are superior to many people in some way, but never get around to fully utilizing your abilities because you are constantly focusing on your failings.

Don't Belong: In this injunction, Mom and Dad don't include the children in their closeness with each other so the child feels like an outsider. This may also be the result of being raised by parents who are suspicious of outside groups. As an adult, you may feel that you don't fit in anywhere.

Don't Want: The child is shamed for wanting anything, sometimes with admonitions that may include making the child feel guilty because they have more than the poor starving children overseas.

Don't Trust: This occurs when the parents are unreliable and cannot be trusted to be there for their children. It also occurs if Mom and Dad are chronically suspicious of other people. As a result, you may grow up feeling anxious and pessimistic and on guard, expecting others to take advantage of you. You may also be overly possessive of your mate and prone to excessive jealousy.

Stop for a minute and consider: Which of these injunctions apply to you? Which ones are currently affecting your life? Try to understand how following these messages may have sabotaged your ability for spontaneous growth. Then consider the next logical question: How is this affecting your relationships, particularly with the person you most want to be close to?

IDENTIFYING YOUR OWN NEGATIVE LIFE RULES

I've found it helpful in my practice to have my patients imagine themselves at five years old and again as a teenager. It is helpful to ask: Where did you live? Can you picture the room you slept in? Can you re-create in your imagination the fragrance of the kitchen or the smells in the bathroom? Was the house a happy, scary, or sad place to be? Who lived there with you?

Imagine your mother talking to you. What's the expression on her face? Do the same with your father, other adults there, your friends and siblings. Feel the response in your body. What emotion are you having? Who is setting the rules? Which of these rules apply to you? What decisions are you making about how to best survive in your family?

CHANGING LIFE HISTORY

1 *Go back again to your childhood scene. This time, give your parents or friends a big transplant of wisdom and unconditional love and change the scene so you feel safe, happy, and wonderful about yourself.*
2 *Make a redecision about yourself and the people around you.*
3 *Imagine the new you following through with the new direction. Imagine how it feels to be unconditionally loved, to be cherished*

and celebrated for the uniqueness of who you are. Imagine that
you are not imagining. You really are the new you!

4 *Go out and practice the new you over and over again, loving*
   yourself more and more each time you do it.

5 *You will probably feel anxious as you do it. Use the Inner Self*
   Meditations you learned earlier to take care of any anxiety
   that occurs (see Chapter 2).

6 *Forgive whoever it was that harmed you intentionally or*
   unintentionally when you were a child. Chances are they
   knew not what they did.

A NOTE ON MEMORY

Old memories are like movies you have seen. Everyone
has a different perspective and conclusion about what
went on. Naturally, you can't change what actually happened
in your past, but you can change your reaction to it by creating a new scene. Every time you have an unpleasant emotion,
it revives old memory traces of similar pain. As a result, any
suffering you experience now is magnified by past experiences. Repeating and changing old history at a conscious
level can help you avoid rubber-banding back to a painful
past. The Inner Self Meditations (see Chapter 2) can help
reduce the intensity and duration of anxiety, sadness, and
anger and eventually channel them into smaller and smaller
parts of your daily life.

CASE VIGNETTE: JOE

I love to tell the story about Joe, my "impatient patient," who scared me more than anyone I ever met. He was a huge man – his muscles literally bulged out of his shirt as he paced angrily back and forth in my office one day. Too agitated to sit down, he shouted at me with astonishing belligerence, "I'm afraid I'll kill someone! I caught myself punching my wife this morning."

Alternating between thoughts of calling the police and frantically thinking of what I could say that might help, I finally relaxed and let myself be with his anger instead of withdrawing in fear. I said, "You certainly have a powerful anger. Sometimes I wish I could be that angry. Where did you learn to do that?" Feeling acceptance lowered his guard and Joe soon calmed down enough to sit in the chair opposite mine.

Subdued and sad, Joe explained, "My dad was angry all the time. He used to beat me up for nothing." This gave me the opportunity to explain to Joe that anger is one of the habits we develop as children to get along in what is often a malevolent world. I then suggested that since he didn't need anger as much as an adult, it would be good for him to learn how to give up anger as a way of handling things. It didn't matter if the anger was justified or not – it was a burden that was destroying instead of helping him.

I was surprised when he replied enthusiastically. "I sure would like to do that. It's done nothing but give me trouble. I broke up my last marriage with it and it keeps getting me fired from jobs."

Forty years old and a deckhand by trade, Joe admitted to having a strong impulse to kill a shipmate who had cheated him out *of $150. Following instructions for the Inner Self Meditation, I asked him to locate where in his body the anger felt strongest and to let a thought come to mind when he first had that kind of angry feeling as a child. He was able to do so immediately. He saw the five-year-old boy scowling. He felt murderous rage toward his father who was drunk and beating him with a belt for talking back. He remembered feeling afraid that his father would kill him.*

Joe's childhood decision was to rebel furiously against the DON'T BE message he was receiving, even though it meant killing someone else to survive. When I asked Joe to turn that scene into one that would make him feel good, he was able to imagine his father affectionately holding a five-year-old Joe and inviting him to play catch. Following instructions for the Inner Self Meditation, Joe held the child in his lap. He breathed in the child's anger and sent him compassion and unconditional love with his out-breath. In a few minutes, Joe reported that the child had calmed down. I encouraged him to go back into the meditation. A few minutes later, a broad smile came over Joe's face. "He's smiling at me!" he exclaimed.

The next time he came to my office, Joe had a beautiful smile on his face. "It works!" he said, excitedly. "My wife and I can't believe the change in me!" Neither could I. I had to restrain my urge to hug him, but in thinking back now I realize maybe I shouldn't have held back. In any event, Joe made an important redecision at that point. "I'm going to give up using anger to get what I want." He settled the problem with his shipmate without provoking a fight.

Many of us have an uncanny knack for choosing a person who will reinforce these induced inhibitions. The relationship might work well for some time, but these injunctions may also fester to the point where they lead to divorce or estrangement from your loved one later in life.

HOW TO CHANGE DESTRUCTIVE RULES FOR LIVING

Someone else saddled you with negative rules for living but you are the one who decided to follow them. It is wonderful to know that you now have the freedom to reverse them. Here are five steps that will help you do that:

1 Identify which injunctions you have been following. How have they affected you emotionally? How have they molded your behavior?
2 Give yourself heartfelt permission to reverse the rules.
3 In your own way, proclaim to the world your new guidelines for living. They might sound like this: I have a right to be alive and to want good things for myself. I have a right to succeed. I can rejoice in having fun! It's good to trust and be close to people!
4 Make a conscious effort to practice the new behaviors. Every day will present you with opportunities to break through those old restrictive habits.
5 If you feel insecure or anxious practicing being 'the new you' repeat the Inner Self Meditation you learned in Chapter 2 to nurture yourself through the change.

HOW TO BECOME MASTER
OF YOUR OWN LIFE

As children, we were subjected to influences and rules from the family. We made the decision whether or not to obey the rules based on our childhood appraisal of how best to get along with the authority figures in the family. As adults, we are in effect often letting that small child who still resides in us tell us how best to lead our lives. I have found it tremendously liberating with myself and my patients to identify and change the rules as we grow in wisdom and experience.

Redeciding

Every minute of your life is an opportunity to redecide to live fully in this moment, the only moment in which we can actually live. This is the reverse of the DON'T BE rule. All of the solutions to the negative rules we identified earlier involve a reversal of your previous thought patterns and behavior. This isn't a rebellion but a joyful proclamation that radiates from your heart, energizing your body to move past the timidity and stagnation of your "stuck" place. Gradually, you'll feel more and more comfortable giving up mistrust and enjoy being who you are, free to play and cherish your own wisdom, go after what you want and relish the pleasures of being intimate.

CASE VIGNETTE: JONATHAN

Jonathan's case is an example of someone who chose a partner who reinforced his injunction, "Don't Want." Jonathan came from a large family. As a child, he was often shamed for wanting anything of his own and for not sharing with his siblings. His wife, Roselyn, meanwhile, was a deeply religious person who frowned on having any material possessions and gave lavishly to charity. Jonathan naturally felt guilty if he bought anything for himself. As the distance between them grew, Jonathan began to resent his wife's open disapproval of any possessions he wanted to buy for himself. Jonathan mentioned that he was resentful because if it weren't for Roselyn, he could buy a motorbike and have a pleasant ride to work instead of struggling with his bicycle on hot days. He would, of course, feel guilty buying the motorbike even if he weren't married to Roselyn, but it was much easier for him to shift the blame to her.

When both of them began to understand how they were shamed into not wanting things for themselves as children, they eventually learned how to be more generous with each other.

The cure for all these suffocating rules is, as you might expect, to *reverse the message*. I am not speaking of rebelling and going completely in the opposite direction – rather I mean that we must make a conscious decision from the heart that it is perfectly okay to be alive and to want good things for ourselves. It is perfectly fine to have fun and not be serious all the time, to be successful and close to other people, to feel your right to belong and to trust. When you attempt to make these changes, you may encounter fear and a deep sense of insecurity. But you can handle this by repeatedly using the Inner Self Meditation you learned in Chapter 2.

POSITIVE DRIVERS

You may, on the other hand, have inherited a number of "positive" drivers or admonitions. These may have been well-meaning but are in fact subtly self-defeating.

Be Perfect: There is no such thing as perfection. If you try to be perfect, you will never enjoy the process of what you are doing because you fear you will not live up to your expectations. No matter how well you do something, you always feel like a failure because you have not lived up to your own impossible goals. It creates a feeling of constant insecurity because you are never "good enough." And it also tends to make you attack people you "love" for being imperfect.

Hurry Up: You are not alright if you can't do things fast enough or on a schedule that pleases someone else. Or perhaps your partner is rushing all the time in order to get on to the next thing in life. You may feel tense just being around people like this because you can't allow yourself to enjoy things at a comfortable pace. This leads to constant fear and anxiety as you set unrealistic goals for accomplishing tasks, and to mistakes that reinforce your feelings of inadequacy.

Be Strong: This one is usually addressed to men but sometimes to women as well. It means you are not supposed to have "weak" feelings. You are expected never to be afraid or sad – and you must certainly never cry. You are often unable to ask for or receive emotional support for yourself or give it to others. If your lover is "strong" and unemotional, you never have a chance to take care of them. Thus you will not have the opportunity to honor the nurturing part of yourself. You may be relegated to the role of the "weak" one.

Please Me: If you act, think, or feel in a way that is not pleasing to Mom and Dad, you are scolded or made to feel guilty because they act hurt. Your life becomes designed to please your parents, and from this you decide that you must please everyone else as well – and feel guilty if you do not. At the extreme, you may spend your life doing this and lose touch with what you really want for yourself. Ask yourself: Can I really be close to anyone if I *have* to please them? Am I afraid they won't love me if I don't live up to their expectations? Intimacy occurs when your decision to please is a heartfelt one.

Try Harder: If you obey this driver, you can never do anything enjoyable or at a natural pace. As with the "Be Perfect" driver, you can never try hard enough.

These messages become drivers for your whole life. Your outer self beats up your inner self into living up to them. You learn to motivate yourself to do things through fear of disapproval if you stray from the admonitions of the drivers. This is a major underlying cause for stress and plays a crucial role in producing physical disease. You exert so much energy following them that there is little left for you to be fully present with the one you love.

It is helpful at this point to pause for a few minutes and determine which of these drivers are affecting you at this moment. Are you reading this book in a relaxed and enjoyable way that enables you to take it in and feel good about it? Are you "trying harder" to understand everything? Are one or more of the drivers pushing you? You will find it easier to explore the issues in later chapters if you can implement the alternatives discussed here. These antidotes to the drivers are your true legacy!

Antidotes to Drivers

Antidote to "Be Perfect": Instead of being perfect, enjoy your own abilities – whatever they are. Since your energy is no longer tied up in your fear of not doing something perfectly, you are able to focus better on what you are doing. Your performance improves and your skill grows at a faster pace due to your increased confidence and enjoyment of the tasks at hand. Your motivation to do something well comes from your satisfaction and pleasure in doing it rather than from a fear of not being perfect. A vast number of circumstances determine how well you will be able to perform a given activity. Things like your past experience and physical fatigue must be considered, along with other important issues in your life which also demand your energy and attention.

Antidote to "Be Strong": It is human to have feelings. You are not a machine. Feelings are necessary in order for you to evaluate your life and change it – to take care of yourself. "Being strong" causes you to obscure your own needs. It also makes you indifferent or unaware of the needs of others because the same drivers you impose on yourself are the ones you many times project on to others – a vicious cycle, to be sure.

Antidote to "Please Me": With the exception of an emergency, you should always consider yourself first. How are you feeling? What are your needs at this moment? And then when you make a decision to please someone else, do it freely and enjoy your contribution to them as a loving act. This does not imply that you are to become selfish. If you decide that your loved ones' needs are more intense than your own, enjoy the pleasure of generously giving and putting your needs on the back burner for the time being.

Antidote to "Try Harder": You will be much more effective and efficient if you take into consideration your own natural physiological, emotional state as you engage in an activity. If you try hard to hit a home run, your body becomes tense and you increase the odds of missing the ball. If you relax and simply enjoy watching the ball come and swing freely, you have a much better chance of succeeding.

RACKETS: ANGER, DEPRESSION, ANXIETY, AND CONFUSION

A "racket" is a term used to describe habitual bad feelings that we learned as a child to deal with difficult situations. We create these feelings in an attempt to remain a child. These habits duplicate the familiar emotions of being in our childhood home, and impair our ability to assume adult responsibilities. The term emphasizes the power we had as a child but didn't know how to use.

Picture a little boy or girl holding an automatic rifle, pointing it at any uncaring parent or other authority figure, saying, in effect: "I'm going to defend myself or mow you down with my fear, sadness, anger, or confusion if you don't love me and stop hurting me or angering me." The result is that we internalize the authority figures and torment our-selves with our own unconscious negative injunctions, or "drivers", and react with the same unhappy emotion we had as a child.

I remember how liberating it was for me when I attended my first lecture on transactional analysis, the psychological approach that introduced the term "rackets." I understood that I produced my own depression and that I had the power to give it up!

You can do the same. Start by making the following con-tract with yourself:

I won't use depression, anxiety, anger, or confusion to deal with problems.

This is not a New Year's resolution! – it is an intention to change. Can you imagine how pleasurable it will be to share love, equanimity, or excitement with your intimate other instead of sadness, fear, or anger? No rackets to put a cork on loving energy.

Being depressed, anxious, or angry with your partner is a form of emotional blackmail or an attempt to manipulate if they don't do what you want them to do. Sharing your income or cleaning the house can be a resentful burden if you have to do it to keep your spouse happy. Conversely, if it stems from a loving and heartfelt decision, it can be a fulfilling pleasure.

EXERCISE

Write down the injunctions and drivers that seem to fit you. Then note those which might belong to your partner. How are they affecting you? How do they keep you from being close? For example, a hug and a kiss when your lover makes a mistake is loving reassurance to their redecision to give up having to be perfect. Talk it over with each other to help both of you give up these old habits. It will take some time to change these life patterns, but the payoff is well worth it. As you become more experienced with the Inner Self Meditation (see Chapter 2) and the technique of Creating a New Life History. You may find it more effective to move directly to creating a new Life History first (see page 40). This is particularly true if the current trauma you are experiencing activates old memory traces that keep you ruminating on pain. Returning to and changing the original source of the pain makes it easier to take care of your inner child as an adult.

CHANGE YOUR TRAGEDY INTO
A ROMANTIC COMEDY

In trying to carry out your script rules, you tend to adopt favorite roles in life that come under the title of persecutor, victim, or rescuer. For example, you need to keep your house perfectly clean and your partner leaves things lying around. The tendency would be to persecute them all the time to keep things immaculate. Your mate ends up feeling like a victim. Or you may make yourself into a victim by having excessive expectations of yourself and not being able to live up to them. And your partner is always coming to your rescue, to reassure you that you are okay.

We can easily shift from one role to another. The victim gets fed up and persecutes their partner for a while, then feels guilty and rescues the person who has been persecuted. A rescuer, for example, may spend their whole life trying to take care of a suicidal partner. The partner is always threatening suicide because they are suffering from a sense of a lack of permission to be alive.

Whenever you are in such roles with each other, you are essentially avoiding intimacy. As we discussed earlier, you eventually end up feeling anxious, afraid, angry, sad, or confused. You play this out with your partner by taking the role of a persecutor, rescuer, or victim. You may think: "I wouldn't be having these bad feelings if you weren't the way you are."

Are you in one or more of these roles with your partner now? If so, congratulate yourself for recognizing it. Laugh at the drama of it all. You can walk off that stage at any time and cuddle with your partner.

A GOAT NAMED LADY MACBETH

Many years later, I'm still astonished by the lessons I learned from a goat named Lady Macbeth. Lady Macbeth lived a tranquil life, free to roam the fields surrounding the Cornell University Behavior Farm where I studied and did research as a student.

She was a dainty white goat with small black horns who loved to hang out with her boyfriend, Tangerine, a broad-shouldered male with great curved horns. All Lady Macbeth and Tangerine had to do in return for their excellent care was to visit a laboratory for training and have their blood pressure checked twice a week.

In the lab, Lady Macbeth easily learned how to lift her right front hoof between the fifth and tenth second of the sounding of a buzzer, thus avoiding a very mild electric shock. All went well until the psychologist who was doing the research started adding weights to her leg, making it more and more difficult to avoid the shock. When she was led into the lab later, instead of calmly chewing her cud as she had done before, Lady Macbeth began to act in a most peculiar fashion.

She would jerk her leg up and down even though no signal had sounded. Apparently she was anticipating the sequence of events, tensing up. One day she had obviously had enough. She let out a tremendous "Baaaaaaaaah!," rolled over on her back with her legs stiffly sticking up and refused to budge. Even a pinprick would not make her move. When tested, her blood pressure had shot up sky high. Suffice it to say that she was probably the most catatonic goat in history.

Have you ever felt like a Lady Macbeth – with so many restrictions or expectations that you felt like giving up? Perhaps you feel that way now – tied down with responsibilities that become so onerous that you feel angry, sad, or frightened. Lady Macbeth's story, however, had a happy ending. After being petted lovingly for several minutes, she stood up, went outside and ran to her beloved Tangerine. Your life story can also have a happy ending.

SUMMARY

This story about Lady Macbeth is germane to us humans, too. Like Lady Macbeth, our freedom is also curtailed by habits and conditioned responses to stimuli. The difference is that we condition ourselves. The signals we respond to automatically are our thoughts, emotions, and physical sensations. These contain our ego and personality.

Most of the thoughts and emotions we have today are identical to the ones we had yesterday and the day before. The origins of these habitual thinking patterns are in childhood where they formed building blocks for our life scripts – a story line that frames how we should live the rest of our lives.

The conditioning lab kept Lady Macbeth from romping in the field with Tangerine. Your life script similarly restricts your freedom in an intimate relationship. Instead celebrate "vive la difference."

The psychotherapy techniques offered in this book will enable you to change decisions you made as a child that dictate your current, adult life script and place major limitations on you. These techniques will also enable you to pinpoint and root out the causes of anger, anxiety, and depression.

Meditation techniques will similarly help you to be mindful of and let go of moment-to-moment thoughts, emotions, and physical responses that keep you tied down now.

The last two chapters have given you the tools to know yourself intimately and to love yourself unconditionally. In turn, this liberates you to do the same with the person you love. Every moment you live is an opportunity for a full and complete rebirth. Do this together with your mate. Your love and romantic feelings will never go stale.

OVERCOMING
THE FEAR OF
INTIMACY

The joy that comes with sharing love can produce an adventure in rapture that is seldom experienced in human relationships. Universally sought, the joy of intimacy is the meat and potatoes of every songwriter, poet, and ad executive. It is our major source of great pleasure and comfort. **But the pleasure of intimacy is often consciously and unconsciously thwarted by fears that may cause us to back away from the very thing we desire.**

ANXIETY – THE HELPFUL GREMLIN

Anxiety is a signal that you are anticipating something bad happening in the future. Often, it appears as if out of nowhere, descending and foreboding. You find yourself closing in and withdrawing. The root cause of fear may be readily identifiable and mild but it can also be intense, with its source not easily seen. But you can relieve anxiety if you recognize its presence and accept it with love and compassion. This is the child part of your personality sending you a message that needs to be listened to. You might have to take a few minutes and use the Inner Self Meditation (see Chapter 2) to make yourself comfortable enough to specifically identify what the fear is about.

Once you know what your fear is about and accept it totally, you can become more comfortable talking about it to your lover. Be as explicit as possible. If your lover is understanding and caring, it paves the way for future closeness. If, on the other hand, their response is less than understanding, it is indicative of the need to pause and evaluate the relationship.

In this chapter we look at some of the most common fears that might cause you and your lover to distance yourselves from each other rather than becoming closer.

How Can You Love Someone Like Me?

Groucho Marx's classic line – "I wouldn't join any club that would accept me as a member" – is appropriate here. Your child mind might say: "I don't love myself so there must be something wrong with you if you want to be close to me." In this scenario, you are being self-critical, and you expect anyone who cares about you to be the same if they really get to know you. Of course, criticizing yourself is bad enough, but when you imagine the person you are attracted to joining in the bashing, it can be overwhelming. At the first sign of anxiety, stop and see if you are being self-critical. Apologize to yourself and love yourself for caring.

Fear of Silence

I recall things going along swimmingly with my new girlfriend, Kari, the vivacious and outgoing woman I would eventually marry. But on our third date, we had been together a couple of hours when, without warning, I perceived a silence that seemed to ominously fill the room. I began to feel anxious. She looked relaxed, but I found myself second-guessing what might be whirling around in her brain. I realized that I was afraid she would find me boring if I had nothing to say. I struggled to think of something interesting but only became more uncomfortable. Finally, I told her exactly how I felt. "I feel anxious about not talking. I'm afraid you won't want to be with me if I'm not more entertaining." She surprised me with a warm smile, replying, "I love being here with you without having to talk. It feels so comfortable."

Fear of Rejection

The fear that you will be deserted usually concerns things you did or did not do in your past, or emotions or habits you may be ashamed of. You might fear rejection because of your family background, your physical appearance, your intelligence, or your character – in short, anything you do not accept in yourself. Unconditional love for yourself as described in Chapters 2 and 3 and letting go of the past are the keys that will keep you from backing away.

CASE VIGNETTE: CASSIE

The following case demonstrates how self-acceptance minimizes the chance of rejection:

Cassie, an attractive divorcée, came into treatment to overcome her fear of going to graduate school. She had little trouble with intimacy, despite the fact she had to deal with having had a mastectomy. Cassie was popular with men and enjoyed being close physically and emotionally. She'd had several long-term affairs and was optimistic that she would eventually find the right one to marry. The mastectomy had taken place approximately ten years before. She had adjusted to having only one breast and did not want plastic surgery. When a new lover start-

ed to fondle her breast she would smile and whisper in his ear, "That one's fake, but the other one is real. I have had a mastectomy." It was reassuring to her that men accepted her body as well as she had.

Fuzzy Boundaries — I'll Lose Me in Pleasing You

If you were raised to please your parents at your expense (see "Please Me" in Chapter 3), there is the very real danger that you will give up being true to yourself in your efforts to please your partner. The reverse may also be true. You may feel hurt or angry if your partner doesn't please you. Over a period of time, you begin to resent having to please. Even worse, you might bury what you want so deeply that you become unable to identify your own needs. The likelihood of this happening is greatest if your partner has a "more important" position in life and/or a more compelling or outgoing personality. Remember that the antidote for this toxic behavior is always to consider your own physical, emotional, and intellectual needs first, and then make a decision about doing something that pleases your partner. Make this an act of loving generosity as opposed to one arising out of fear.

I'll Become Too Dependent on You: Interdependence

You cherish being with your partner. Even going to the grocery store with your mate is fun. You amble down one aisle and your spark in life goes down the next. Each of you is on a treasure hunt for what you need or for some surprise treat. One of you gets lost in the aisles. You have a double prize in the store – the smile that comes from finding each other again and sharing what you've found. This is interdependence at its best. It is caring, helpful, enjoyable, immensely rewarding on a deep level. You do need each other and rely upon each other for many, many things.

The Myth of Independence

The myth of independence is just that – a myth, and a dangerous one at that. How many people were involved in getting you that cup of coffee this morning? There are the farmers and workers who planted and harvested the beans on that misty mountainside in South America. There was also a farmer who grew the hemp and the workers at the manufacturing plant who produced the material and stitched together the sack to store and transport the coffee beans. And then the scores of people who drive the trucks or pilot the ships that bring the coffee to this country. Then there's the roaster who grinds and packages the coffee and the clerks at the stores who sell it to you or the waitresses at coffee shops who serve it to you. So go back and slowly savor another cup – but this time be thankful and grateful for the hundreds of people who worked so hard bringing it to you.

Now, do the same thing with the love of your life. Think of all that you love about them. Make a list of all the things you need and receive from them, both practical and emotional. Feel and express gratitude for each one, every time you think about it. Have your partner do the same for you. Enjoy the comfort that comes from interdependence.

The small child in us loves to be taken care of. As we discussed in Chapter 3, some of us receive the script message,

"Don't grow up." Following that dictum, we avoid being competent and feel helpless. Along comes someone who thrives on being a caretaker and you are hooked on your own helplessness. Paradoxically, many people avoid intimacy because they have a very strong desire to be taken care of but fear becoming helpless. They are so terrified of losing the person they want to cling to that they actually reject them.

CASE VIGNETTE: VIRGINIA

Virginia, over-protected as a child, married Ray, who was a highly responsible adult – and had been since he was ten years old. He'd had to grow up quickly because his child-like parents were too busy playing or fighting to pay attention to him. Ray advised Virginia about everything. He had warm and caring feelings for her but didn't know how to express them. She did not hesitate to call him frequently about the trivial problems of her everyday life. If she had a flat tire, he would leave work to rescue her. Virginia became more and more depressed. She despised Ray for "not having feelings." In desperation, she fell in love with another man – one she believed to be a happy playboy – but this made her feel even more helpless and depressed. She did not have the strength to give up her lover who provided her with romantic fun, or give up Ray who "had no faults and took such good care" of her.

I was called on to help her from the hospital where she'd been taken after an overdose of pills in a suicide attempt. It took two years to help Ray and Virginia untangle the mess they'd made of their relationship. Eventually, they both decided it was best to *divorce. But since that time, Virginia has learned to access her own strengths and to gain a healthy sense of self-sufficiency. Ray, meanwhile, ultimately learned how to enjoy his emotions and avoid being trapped as a super caretaker.*

I Feel Like I've Been Skinned Alive – The Fear of Sharing Emotions

Earlier in my career, when I was practicing psychoanalysis, a forty-year-old physician was lying on the couch, rambling on with complaints about his wife's complaints. He told me that she was always angry with him for not being affectionate enough. For his part, he said he gave her all the money he earned and had sex with her once a week – or more if she wanted. "I don't know what she expects," he complained.

Frequently during our sessions, I would interrupt his emotionless diatribes by asking him very simply: "What are you feeling now?" His answers were often detailed dissertations about his thoughts, without any hint of emotion. One day, he dutifully reported a dream he'd had the previous night. As he described it, "Some natives tied me up and started to skin me alive. Then I woke up."

I awakened from my usual boredom with his dull and monotonous delivery, not from the horror of the dream, but by his suddenly sitting up and staring angrily at me. "That's how I feel!" he exclaimed. His words were like bullets. Since that day, I have learned to feel deep empathy and caring for anyone who has difficulty sharing their emotions.

Remember this story whenever you feel your partner is emotionless. Emotions, after all, are disciplined or beaten out of most males in kindergarten – that is, if they haven't been squashed sooner at home. I remember being terrified as a three-year-old boy when the pony I was on galloped off with inexperienced me on its back. My father's obnoxious command: "Be a man, stop whimpering," made me feel even worse. But his advice may have kept me from the ridicule suffered by some of my kindergarten peers who were taunted as crybabies if they showed the slightest fear.

What to Do with a Partner Who Doesn't Share Emotions

You cannot be intimate with someone who does not share your feelings or, even worse, does not seem to have feelings. So what do you do with that person you married because they looked so strong, brave, competent, and stoic? Start by asking your partner to read this part of the chapter. Explain very gently that you love them, and each time they share a feeling there is more of them to love. Assure your partner that there is no need to be tough as nails to earn your love. If you are the one who is hobbled by being the strong, tough one, don't be defensive about this process. You have done a great job surviving in a brutally tough culture. But sharing your emotions will put you in a position to have a much fuller life.

HOW TO IDENTIFY HIDDEN EMOTIONS

Do the following as many times as necessary each day until emotions, especially the positive and exciting ones, flow out of you like a breath of fresh air.

- ❖ *Ask yourself: What am I feeling right now?*
- ❖ *Identify a tension or pressure somewhere in your body. Imagine part of you bursting to let out some feeling and label it as sexy, excited, happy, loving, anxious, scared, angry, confused, or whatever term seems appropriate.*
- ❖ *You may feel a little anxious at this point. Reassure yourself that you will not let anything disastrous happen and express the emotion out loud.*
- ❖ *Celebrate your victory. You've just "hit one out of the park" in expressing your feelings.*

Taming the Beast – Unleashed Anger

If the emotion is anger, be happy you can identify it. If you are not used to expressing anger, it can feel like an atomic bomb, ready to explode. Practice expressing it *away* from your partner at first. Enjoy screaming, "I'm furious!" in your car or pounding your fist against a pillow as you let it out. Yell at the top of your lungs. You might also muffle the sound as you scream into a pillow. Enjoy feeling the power of it. Roar like a lion – let yourself be your anger! Remember this anger is yours – own it, enjoy the power of it, but *don't* use it against your lover. The purpose of doing these anger exercises is simply to become comfortable with anger and let it go.

When you are comfortable with your anger, use one of the techniques described in Chapter 10 to transform its destructive energy into effective power. You can now use that power to negotiate effectively with your partner to examine and deal with whatever offended you. We are all hardwired by genetic inheritance with a beast inside. It is a wonderful trait to be able to use our inner beast's power for positive living. Following the "No Anger" contract (see page 138) is extremely important here. You work together with your mate to solve problems instead of becoming enemies.

Sexy You?

When you feel happy with someone, the positive energy goes through your body. Your endorphins flow. Testosterone and estrogen levels increase. All of your body is stimulated with pleasure, including your sexual organs. If you were raised to believe it was bad to be sexy or had traumatic sexual experiences in the past, rising anxiety comes back in to block your intimacy. You withdraw rather than moving closer.

The anxiety represents a conflict between desire and fear. Your inner and outer selves are battling it out. One part of you says, "My partner is wonderful and sexy. I am so excited. I can't wait to go to bed with them." Another part says, "He is just after sex," or "She just wants to seduce and control me," or "How many lovers has he had in the past?" or

"You're going to get hurt." Add to that the fears of being criticized or rejected by your lover for real or imagined imperfec-
tions in your body or sexual performance, and your anxiety
often escalates.

Sex – A Mirror of Emotional Intimacy

I have had patients who over and over again begin to have a
good relationship and break it off as sensuality comes into
play. Sexy feelings are avoided by withdrawing. Others bury
their anxiety about intimacy by plunging into a frenzy of pas-
sionate sexuality without getting close emotionally with their
partner. How free you feel about talking about or enjoying
your lover is a mirror that reflects your level of emotional
intimacy.

WHAT TO DO ABOUT IT

✤ *Don't back away from your sensual feelings by withdrawing.*
✤ *Don't brush your anxiety aside by hopping into bed.*
✤ *Do respect your anxiety by using the Inner Self Meditation.
(There is much more on this in Chapter 8, "The Zen of
Sexuality.")*

In the meantime, simply love yourself for caring. The following procedure will help to remove your anxiety:

✤ Remember having feelings of love for someone or something? Breathe those feelings in. Breathe them out. Experience the love you are producing.

✤ Shift the loving feelings to your self. Each time you breathe in, open up the space around your heart with total acceptance. As you breathe out, love your self for caring about yourself and others.

✤ When you feel comfortable, talk about your fears with your partner. Their understanding and compassion deepens your closeness.

If your partner is critical, it is an indication that further work needs to be done on developing emotional intimacy before venturing into a sexual relationship.

The Fear of Being Controlled

Control is a major area of conflict in many relationships. Instead of being devoted to the integrity and happiness of our partner, we want to control how they think or act to match our own standards or needs.

But I'm Only Trying to Help You

Ray, the bemused husband we talked about earlier, gave caring advice to Virginia and came to her rescue by taking care of things she could really manage on her own. A part of his motivation was caring, which he could not express emotionally.

The dark cloud under this silver lining was control. In Ray's profession, excellence came from taking meticulous care of details. The sense of anxiety that permeated their relationship was a foreboding signal of ongoing damage. Ray was getting more and more lost in his futile need to control everything, and Virginia was drowning in her conflicting desires to be independent and to be taken care of.

It can be difficult to tell the difference between control and caring. For the person trying to stop controlling, it involves giving up perfectionist expectations, expecting your partner to do things the way you do. For the person being controlled, it involves giving up having to please and facing the fear of being responsible. It requires being aware of the difference between the anxious, heavy feeling of being dependent and the light, loving security of interdependence. In the back of our minds lingers the ghost of Mom and Dad, who are there to take care of us. The person who is dependent transfers that expectation to their partner.

What to Do About It

If you are the person controlling, recognize and talk about it. There is no right or wrong here. If you are accused of being controlling, accept that fact as your partner's reality and invite them to alert you to it at the time it occurs. Don't argue about it. Put yourself in their shoes and try to understand the message you are sending out.

The following meditation can be used whenever you have the impulse to tell your lover what to do, give advice without being asked, or feel impatient with them. It will free you to love them as they are.

If you are the person being controlled, see if you are inviting it by not being responsible and by being overly dependent upon your mate. Recognize that being sad or scared to do something is your inner self blackmailing your lover to do something you don't want to do. Recognize that as dependency you no longer need. The meditation that follows will free you to love on an adult level.

MEDITATION TO ERASE HAVING TO CONTROL OR BEING DEPENDENT

❖ *Identity your impulse to control or need to be dependent.*

❖ *Feel love and excitement for yourself for recognizing and deciding to change it.*

❖ *Watch your breath. As you watch your abdomen rise with each inhalation and fall with each exhalation, you will become aware of a torrent of thoughts – some foreboding, some angry, some fearful.*

❖ *Be aware of any tension in your body and let it relax with each exhalation.*

❖ *Identify emotions that arise – anxiety, anger, fear, sadness, confusion – and take care of them by using the Inner Self Meditation (see Chapter 2) or simply being caringly aware of each emotion as it rises and falls in intensity, returning to your breath as the pathway to inner peace.*

❖ *You will notice that your need to be the boss or your need to be taken care of has diminished. Send unconditional loving energy to your partner with each breath as you feel grateful for the qualities in them that you cherish.*

❖ *Give them a hug and celebrate their aliveness, loving them as they are instead of coercing them to please you.*

Under the new umbrella of unconditional caring, adapting to each other's differences will be a loving act instead of a response to coercion.

SUMMARY

We covered some fears that rise to the surface like alligators in a romantic lagoon. Being aware of them is the first step to avoid the danger of being hurt. Anxiety and physical tension alert you to their submerged presence. Practicing the meditation suggested will tame them. Now that you have made it safe to be close, your lover has become very important in your life. What kind of commitment are you ready to make to each other? Chapter 5 will help you sort those questions out.

COMMITMENT:
JAIL OR
PLAYPEN?

CASE VIGNETTE: YUPPIE LOVE

Antoine is a good-looking forty-year-old lawyer. He enjoys his yuppie life, taking his corporate clients to lunch, playing hard at nightlife. Outgoing and popular, he has a social calendar filled with invitations to parties where pot, cocaine, and beautiful women circulate in abundance.

Antoine came to me because, for some unknown reason, he began feeling anxious and depressed. He spent most of his initial session telling me entertaining stories about his work, his affairs, his party life. Antoine was a wonderful storyteller and I enjoyed listening until I realized that I was enjoying it too much. I began to feel guilty for not earning my fee.

I expressed sincere appreciation for his panache and his great storytelling ability and asked him: "What needs fixing?"

Antoine's 6'3" frame shrank into his beautifully tailored suit. He was sad, scared, and confused. Tired of putting on a front, Antoine doubted if there was anything about him that was real.

Antoine's identity crisis was brought on by a growing sense of emptiness. Nothing he did had any real meaning. This feeling reached a peak with his growing attachment to a woman we'll call "Claire." He suspected, correctly, that he was having sincere loving feelings for her, and she for him. Unavoidably, he felt anxious and confused. Most confusing of all was the fear he had when he thought of having sex with her. He admitted that he was physically attracted to her – with an intensity that was new to him. This was not, I learned, Antoine's usual seduction act. How and when, he asked, do you follow through on such feelings when you really care about someone?

Antoine's innocence and naiveté touched me. It was like talk-ing to a 13-year-old boy who desperately wanted to be good. When he went to parties alone, he missed her. When she did go with him, he avoided drugs. He then began to wonder what he had liked about his friends, especially now that their superficial banter seemed to be intruding on his growing intimacy with Claire. For the first time, he had no interest in dating other women.

Antoine, we discovered, was trapped by love!

To begin a close relationship does require giving up some other people and activities. The key to feeling good about it is that you are making a wonderful free choice to create more love in your life.

COMMITMENT TO WHAT?

As you get to know a person as someone you really enjoy being with, commitment becomes more and more of an issue. Unless you make conscious decisions that balance your needs with those of your lover, you may start to feel trapped because *you invest more and more of your time and energy in the relationship*, and attend less and less to yourself as an independent entity.

The feeling of being trapped sometimes manifests itself in second-guessing your commitment: But, you might think to yourself, someone better may come along!

This is a reality you must face as you think of giving up dating other people. It is, in fact, true: there is always someone out there who is smarter, more attractive, wealthier, funnier, more lively, or may possess any number of more appealing characteristics than the person to whom you have made a commitment. You can spend the rest of your life looking for them and still end up alone – and lonely.

But Antoine was trapped by love! My challenge was to help him focus on what was important in his life.

What was he living for? He had to re-examine his sense of values. Could he learn to enjoy living with those values as they changed, as they certainly do throughout life? Could he come to terms with his growing realization that a long-term loving relationship was his primary goal at this time? In the process of answering those questions, Antoine began to grow more and more excited about making his time with Claire his top priority.

In other words, Antoine had made a commitment.

COMMITMENT WHEN ROMANCE FADES: WE LOVE EACH OTHER. NOW WHAT?

So much of our life is spent looking for the right person to love us that we feel at a loose end when the search is over. There is a sense of loss – the highs and lows of the search itself are missing. Now that you've found that person who really matches your expectations, the excitement that came from *desiring something in the future* is no longer there.

If that is true for you, you have not learned how to enjoy life in this moment – the only moment in which you can truly be alive. You have returned to being what the Buddhists describe as a hungry ghost. Your mind is elsewhere, leaving your body as a corpse. You do not feel excited, you may realize, to be with your lover.

In such cases, your responses to your lover's ardent expression of love sound hollow, even to you. Sex may revive things for a while, but that too loses its luster. Guilt creeps in. You start to distance yourself. Like a dog locked in a run, you want to jump the fence and sniff out other possibilities. You may start to resent your new playmate for being controlling when he or she wants to be with you more often. Love turns to anger and you begin to focus on each other's faults to justify your anger. Old habits, pressed into existence by the way you've lived your life, resurface in familiar ways.

OVERCOMING COMMITMENT ANXIETY AND WHAT TO DO ABOUT IT

There are several techniques that can help you overcome this sense of "commitment anxiety:"

1 *You can start by practicing the Inner Self Meditation (see Chapter 2) to help shed any burgeoning fear, sadness or anger. Move back into this moment – the only moment, you must remember, in which you can live – and love yourself. Seize the feeling of how you are at this moment, a moment in which you feel peaceful.*

2 *From that peaceful place, you will learn to recognize whether or not you may be succumbing to old fears – fear of abandonment, perhaps, or fear of missing out on other, presumably "better" opportunities.*

3 *Confront the fears of intimacy detailed in the last chapter and take care of them.*

4 *With that done it's time to make a commitment to yourself, your new love, and the relationship, a commitment that embraces the wellbeing of you both and strengthens your relationship at the same time.*

COMMITMENT IN ACTION

In the third week of my budding relationship with Kari, who ultimately became my wife, I received a startling phone call from a woman who was a stranger to me. Her voice was stern and admonishing. "I'm Kari's best friend. She says she's crazy about you. I don't want to see her hurt. What are your intentions?"

At first I was offended. I really liked Kari. I was excited about seeing her again but it was much too early for me to plan a serious relationship. I withheld my kneejerk reaction to cut her friend off and replaced it with admiration for her courage and caring in calling me. It took a few minutes to come up with an answer that was as close to the truth as possible. The reply coming from my heart was: "I want to explore our relationship to find out how deeply I can learn to love her." That was the commitment I was able to make at that time and one that continues to this day. The commitment was to act in a way that would enhance love in our togetherness. It has worked well for me. I invite you to use it. The commitment represents an open-ended decision to consider the loving best interests of both of you in your future actions and behavior. The specific parameters of your commitment change as your relationship evolves. Let's talk about some of the major ones.

How Much Time Should We Spend Together?

In the beginning, spend enough time to go past your initial superficial appraisals of each other. Is this someone you enjoy being with? Can you find interesting things to talk about? Can you solve problems that come up between you reasonably? Can you alternate the roles of caretaker and being taken care of as the need arises? Do you have similar ethical and moral standards? If your answer to all of these questions is yes, your relationship has great potential.

Friend or Lover?

You may decide that you would like to be friends with that person, but not lovers. Think about this and discuss it in terms of what you like about each other. Celebrate your friendship rather than disappointedly drifting apart. Neither of you is a failure if you don't serve as a sparkplug for romance and sex. You can practice all of the intimacy skills we are talking about with each other. Not having a sexual relationship makes it less complicated and less threatening. I met a friend I hadn't seen for several years. He was uncharacteristically buoyant and happy, ecstatic about his marriage. Neither he nor his wife had been attracted to each other. They liked hanging out together. Love and romance blossomed out of their friendship, despite their lack of chemistry together.

Commitment to Joy

It is common in long-term relationships for couples to take each other for granted. Like the sidewalk in front of your house, you walk on your relationship without paying much attention to it. It looks solid from the outside and all you have to do is sweep it up a bit to make it presentable. You avoid noticing the cracks caused by the roots of trees growing until you trip over them. Children, work, hobbies, and other things figure more prominently in your life and leave little time to notice or nurture your partner.

Investing in a Joyous Relationship

Making a commitment to joy requires nurturing each other every day with appreciation and care. Opening your heart enthusiastically to the miracle of your togetherness each time you see each other and having fun together every day turns a good relationship into a fantastic one. It's never too late to take the time to do that.

Monogamy? When?

At the start of a new relationship you will probably not be ready to give up old ones. Be honest, non-defensive, and caring when the subject comes up. Bring it up when you begin to feel uncomfortable about dating others. As you enjoy being with this person more and more, dating others puts a cautionary damper on new love. You won't like the imposition on your time together or the insecurity that results.

Commitment to Love

"I only have eyes for you dear." A pretty song, but I regret to say, largely unrealistic. Our physiology is hardwired to survival of the species. It's natural for you to want to do your part with attractive people who come your way – even the Bible says, "Love thy neighbor as you do yourself." Because of this, making a commitment to be with one person requires a heart-felt decision that goes against the grain of your inner adolescent – but the rewards in the currency of love are beyond measure.

Loving each other exclusively is a big step forward and a necessary one to give deep intimacy a chance. When you have an urge to stray, remember your commitment not to do anything that will hurt your partner. The guilt, insecurity, and jealousy it will produce are hardly worth any transient pleasure you might obtain. **When you do feel an emotional tug toward someone else, it's okay to enjoy your excitement, then stop and love yourself for not following through with the impulse.**

"Lust but Don't Leap" in Chapter 11 tells you how your interest in being with someone else can represent a need to stoke the fires of your home hearth. That chapter has some exciting information to help you keep the monotony out of monogamy.

COMMITMENT: THE PAUSE THAT REFRESHES AND CAN LAST A LIFETIME

Feel the relief of having made a commitment like the marathon runner who can finally put his legs up on the recliner and sip a cool drink – you can stop running, stop searching, give up the daily pain of loneliness. Feel the power of saying, "At last my love has come along." It feels so good. You are now making a commitment. Give your explorations of each other time to find out how your caring can grow. Feel the security of knowing you are there for each other now – you're not jumping ahead to the future or tied to the past. Commitment is the vital oxygen for intimacy. **It is necessary for its growth and survival. When it is inspired by love, commitment is an exciting plunge into life at its best.**

ADDICTION
TO BEAUTY

What is an addiction to beauty? A poem entitled *The Decision* illustrates the seductiveness that an addiction to beauty may have for many people:

> *Raven hair, waving their cascades of beauty*
> *Over cheekbones and body that could*
> *Inspire generations of warriors.*
> *Paralyzed by her loveliness*
> *I am speechless for a moment that stretches into eternity.*
> *Deep pools of violet eyes pierce my soul with inquiry.*
> *A decision to be made:*
> *do I enter the war of desire,*
> *with its battles of jealousy, control and painful longing*
> *or will I use the radiance of her beauty to guide me*
> *Inwardly,*
> *Polishing my soul with gratefulness for*
> *all that is beautiful within me –*
> *Including my ability to cherish the way she looks.*

As I wrote that poem, I realized it applies to the idea that beauty, or handsomeness, can be used to facilitate intimacy if it is used delicately, to ignite that which is tender and lovely within ourselves. If you water and feed a rosebush with love and care, it rewards you with bigger blossoms and fragrances that delight the air around it. A rose pulled carelessly from its stem withers rapidly. If you become seduced by desire to control a beautiful person, that face contorts into the ugliness of anger, depression, or despair compounded by the helpless sadness over beauty's impermanence. This chapter is designed to help us reverberate to the beauty of others, with a deepening of the beauty within ourselves.

NATURE'S BOOBY TRAP, CULTURE'S PRIDE

"I know I shouldn't be so superficial, but I am." I've heard that sentiment often in my practice. The truth is, however, that we all are suckers for beauty to a greater or lesser extent. Even if it's not an addiction where we compulsively seek out someone who is spectacular to look at, and then become restless and agitated until we land that beautiful fish, that impulse can nevertheless exert a powerful influence over the way we behave. We are all victims, more or less, of the same plot – a veritable double whammy from nature and culture. Our primary job as a species is to reproduce. Nature facilitates that by providing people who are attractive to us. Our culture has added to this mightily by becoming even more adept at merchandising beauty than license plates. One out of a thousand people is chosen to be the epitome of desirability. The unspoken message our culture sends is that if you own, and especially if you can touch, that most wanted person, then you too are desirable. The cure lies in being able to identify specifically the quality you are attracted to and find a way to activate it in yourself – without changing your appearance.

WHAT TURNS YOU ON?

(Chapter 11,"Finding the Cure in the Lure," goes into considerable detail on this topic; we simply mention some points here.)

Physical Factors

If you feel unattractive, it's much nicer to look at someone who's pretty or handsome than to look into the mirror. If you feel basically weak, you want someone who looks strong. If you are a perfectionist, you may continuously search for that perfect-looking man or woman.

Sexual Factors

Looking sexy has become the coin of the realm in many cultures, including our own. It leads to confusion about intimacy and counterfeit love. Chapter 8, "The Zen of Sexuality," will help you transform desire into a powerful force that enhances intimacy instead of destroying it.

Emotional Factors

The woman who is lively and vivacious seems beautiful to an inhibited man. That same quiet, inhibited man may be very attractive to the lady who is tired of expending so much energy.

Spiritual Factors

Great spiritual leaders have hordes of followers, some turned on like bobby-soxers. The meaningfulness of the spiritual message they receive reverberates through their brain and body. Accustomed to sexualizing anything exciting, the followers perceive the spiritual teacher as a sexual object. Instead of taking in his wisdom, they want to take over his body.

CASE VIGNETTE: MILDRED

A patient of mine I'll call Mildred fell in love with her pastor, Jonathan. Jonathan was a genuine man of God, caring and deeply spiritual. Mildred felt very strongly attracted to him. Because she was married, Jonathan encouraged her to look deeply into her unhappiness with her husband. Mildred realized that she longed to find more of a spiritual base for her life. When she verbalized this to her husband, she was amazed to find him intrigued by her search. Their spiritual quest together added new depth to their intimacy.

THE MYTH OF POSSESSING
A BEAUTIFUL WOMAN OR
HANDSOME MAN

If I had that gorgeous person I'd be happy, powerful, turned on, complete, beautiful, and secure. That's what the storybooks tell us, and many people pursue beauty with those goals in mind. The truth is that you might have all those good feelings – at least transiently – with that beautiful person securely attached to your arm. You can get the same high by buying an expensive car. Like the car, your possession becomes old and less interesting. **Love that is powered by the desire to control beauty produces hot passion that dies out quickly unless unconditional love of the deeper qualities within respark the fire.**

WHEN BEAUTY FADES OR ISN'T
THERE IN THE FIRST PLACE

One of my patients described his dilemma over his wife in painful detail. Jack's voice was so soft I could barely hear him. His hands and face were contorted by guilt and despair. He began, "The sweet innocence of her voice touched my heart, as it always has for the past twenty-five years. But then I looked up and was horrified by my reaction to her wrinkled skin and graying hair. It felt hypocritical to tell her I love her, even though somewhere deep down I knew I still felt that way. I couldn't stand the conflict inside of me. How do you tell someone you love, who has been the pivot of your life for many years, that you can't stand the way she looks and you want a divorce? I feel so worthless. I'd rather be dead than face this."

There was a similar theme in an attractive woman, twenty-five years younger. "Rebecca's" legs pumped nervously up and down, as if they were trying to run away from the anxiety and tears in her voice. "Herbert is great. He's fun to be with. He loves kids, earns a good living, just the kind of guy I've been looking for for years. I'm thirty-two – the clock is running out for babies. He'd be a perfect father, but I'm just not turned on by him. His nose is too long; his legs are too thin. I feel broken-hearted about my decision to break off and not see him again. I'm afraid I will never find anyone half as nice as he is."

How many times have I heard the same lament? I love him/her, but I'm not attracted anymore. Here's a meditation you can use when that conflict arises in you.

MEDITATION THAT CURES THE ADDICTION TO BEAUTY AND ENABLES YOU TO LOVE THE PERSON WITHIN

Simple as this meditation appears to be, it has worked with numerous people, men and women, young and old.

1 *You notice yourself withdrawing. You have a critical reaction to some physical aspect of the person you are trying to love, or may have loved before.* Don't verbalize your disdain! *Accept this reaction as you would a dark cloud passing by. You are interested in it, but not attached to it. Let it go, and focus on your breathing.*

2 *Go back in time and recall having a loving feeling. It could be for anyone, even a pet. Open your heart and breathe in that feeling, sending it back out to your intended lover. As you do this, recall some aspect about them that is particularly endearing or admirable. It could be physical, intellectual, emotional, or spiritual. Let the love permeate your entire body, spreading like a warm wave from your heart, and send it out to them. Repeat this process every time you think about or are with your lover. Eventually they will become the epitome of beauty to you. Allow your love to flow freely, physically, through your body, to this person, who more than deserves it.*

TRUE BEAUTY IS A MATTER
OF THE HEART

A s suggested by the poem at the beginning of this chapter, how we react to a person we are attracted to can be seen as a decision. This results in a behavior that can either nurture intimacy and love, or destroy it. It is worthwhile repeating the fact that passion based on desire to possess is accompanied by the need to control – to have things your way. That kind of love is very conditional: "I will only give love to you if you look and act in a certain way." These expectations always lead to disappointment and suffering. How can you turn desire into heartfelt caring, which is a prelude to love that lasts? The meditation that follows will enable you to do that:

TURNING DESIRE INTO CARING
AND LOVE

Imagine meeting someone who is drop-dead gorgeous, or unbelievably handsome.

1. *Stop and become mindful of your staring that heralds desire and then focus on your breathing. Breathing in and breathing out, I am aware of desire energizing my body.*
2. *As you continue to focus on your breathing, send yourself loving enthusiasm, celebrating the vitality of your animal aliveness.*

3 *Continue to focus on your breath, and loving yourself, even more for being mindful of your desire, and not using it to defile the other person with possessiveness.*

4 *Focus on your body. Notice any physical tensions you are having – without labeling them or judging them as good or bad. Watch the tensions rise, fall, or stay the same. Let them go.*

5 *Feel the equanimity of higher self as you breathe, watching yourself smiling gently as you experience joy for the other person's radiant beauty. Love yourself for your ability to appreciate beauty.*

6 *As you breathe, feel your caring more and more intensely for yourself and the other person. Love the radiance of your own caring as it touches the radiance of the beautiful person.*

7 *The way is now open for you to get to know each other in a manner that is unobstructed by past conditioning. You can let the caring feelings flow freely back and forth, and enjoy intimacy with the whole person in front of you.*

SUMMARY

In this chapter, we learned how to be with beauty instead of trying to possess it. This brings up similar questions concerning romance. Why is it so transient? Is it real or fantasy? How can we sustain it for decades instead of letting it disappear in a few weeks or months? Read on and find out!

ROMEO
AND JULIET
WITHOUT
THE TRAGEDY

ADDICTION TO ROMANCE

S ound the trumpets and herald the good news! If you are a romance addict, you don't have to give it up. Here come some ways of bringing it back into your relationship.

Let's talk about elephants. Did you ever see a movie about a herd of elephants traveling in a large group? The biggest and strongest ones are on the outside; the weaker ones are on the inside. Our mammalian cousins take care of each other.

We, too, are born with an instinct to stay together and care for each other. Our long childhood, with its dependency on others, deepens our instinctual need for closeness to others. A baby seeks out its mother before there is a concept of an "I" and a "You." A deep feeling of comfort occurs when the baby is together with its loving mother. Deep inside us there remains a yearning for the comfort of closeness to others. We are hardwired to bond in a loving relationship.

A Cultural Hoax that Erodes Real Relationships

In our culture, this natural desire for closeness has been shoved into a very narrow corner called "Romance." Watch any movie, click on the TV, or read most books and you'll see at the core of many of these stories is a tale of romance longed for, but many times lost. Even the cartoons for young children are romantically directed when they are not being violent. Falling in love with someone is the ideal goal – it provides a rush of excitement, fulfilling a wonderful dream with this perfect image of one's ideal love. This is usually tied in with sexual attractiveness. Our desire for closeness is inexorably squeezed into a narrow range. We are left with a craving for sex and romance. Anything else is too often secondary, or an afterthought.

Our culture gives only a passing nod to maternal love and caring among relatives and friends. It is nice when it happens, the cultural mavens tell us, but it is nothing one is particularly encouraged to pursue. Men and women are taught to seek romance and/or sex. The unspoken message is that unless you succeed on that level, you cannot claim success as a fulfilled man or woman.

A Kindergarten Romance

The pressure for romance starts at an early age. Everyone can empathize with memories of the pain of the first day of school. I clearly remember my first experience in kindergarten. My eyes were still wet with tears from saying goodbye to my mother. I was, in my child's mind, unsure whether she was coming back. I walked up to the piano in the middle of the room where the teacher was plinking out a nursery school tune. I watched the other children. All at once I saw her: a little girl with long, black, wavy hair, dark and shiny eyes, and amazingly fair skin. At the age of five, I'd fallen hopelessly in love with Rhoda. I spent much of my school time that year mooning over her, following her around.

My crush lasted into the first grade, when the teacher assigned Rhoda to be my penmanship partner because her script was perfect and mine was a mess. My heart pounded so hard that I thought everyone in the class could hear it thumping as I sat close to her, hunched over my practice paper. I was so embarrassed by her presence that, much to my humiliation, I carefully copied her name instead of my own. My romantic passion was safely secured in my dream world. I was unable to summon up enough courage to talk to her. Attachment to my mother and the fear of being abandoned that first day in school and for the following year was softened by my attachment to my romantic fantasy. I was, as you can see, a romantic at age five.

The Origin of Addiction to Romance

At that early age and for many years after, I did not know how to appreciate and love myself. Instead, I longed for someone to love me. People who are addicted to romance do just that. As children, we are not accepted for who we are. We didn't obtain the unconditional love from our family that would have given us the emotional security necessary for future relationships. The message "You are fine and wonderful just the way you are" is necessary for each of us to hear. This knowledge is required for us to be able to have loving feelings, not longing feelings, which are painful and destructive.

Our script messages discussed in Chapter 3 produce a relentless demand to become an image we can never attain. We switch to a romantic fantasy that someone else who is a desirable image will fall in love with us – if they love us we can feel lovable. Thus the bait for a romantic addiction is set.

THE GENTLE TRAP

Who you fall in love with is determined by a complex set of stimuli. Physically, it can have something to do with how your mother or father looked or did not look – even the smell of their body can play a part. It might have been affected by your idea of how the opposite sex was presented in a movie, or by whom your peers thought was a hunk or a babe in high school. The more unsatisfied you are with your own appearance, the more compelling it will be to find a more perfect physical image to fall in love with. If you snare that person to be yours alone, you somehow believe you become more attractive. You will learn a great deal more about this in Chapter 11, "Finding the Cure in the Lure."

A Need to Love

A fundamental requirement for being happy is the experience of loving. You rarely think of this as a need, but it is one of our most basic requirements. Healthy growth requires improving your physical, emotional, and intellectual skills, *and increasing your capacity to love*. Those who enjoy life the most love someone or something – and often both – most of the time. Romantic love provides that for us until we see the real person inside that glowing halo we put around them. Then we face the challenge of loving the real person within.

CASE VIGNETTE: LAURA

L aura is an example of a woman who is co-dependent and addicted to romance. Visualize her as she walks into my office: tall, attractive, and vivacious. She delights others with her every word and facial expression. She easily makes a compliment about the way the room is decorated. It is as if she is here to put you at your ease.

She smiles elfishly and says, "I'm going through a rough time; my husband left me." You instinctively know that remark should evoke sympathy, but looking at her and listening to her voice makes it impossible. She is busy entertaining and taking care of me rather than really letting me be with her. "My husband," she continues, "calls three or four times a day since he moved out. I am really worried about him. I know he is miserable, but he won't tell me. Sometimes he is very curt on the phone – he's just trying to get me to do something for him, like pay a bill. He asks how I am, but doesn't seem to care."

Over and over again, I ask Laura how she feels when her husband calls. She keeps replying, "I don't know how to feel. I can't figure him out. He left me, but he keeps calling." What Laura really does not know is how she is feeling. For so many years she has been taking care of the child part of her husband or other men instead of her own feelings. She has lost touch with her own emotions.

In the next session, I taught Laura how to pay attention to her body's sensations as she imagined talking to her husband. She experienced fulness in her chest. I asked her to breathe into her chest. She finally started crying and said she was sad. I instructed her to focus on that area more intensively, to imagine herself as a little girl inside her chest, to imagine reaching in and lifting her out and putting her on her own lap.

"What is the expression on the little girl's face?" I asked.

"Sad," she replied. She looks at the floor, not at me. She is hiding her face. She does not want me to see how she feels.

"Stay with that and accept that in little Laura," I told her. "Hold her and let her know you understand how hard it is for her to show her feelings and that it is okay with you. Just hold her and love her in her sadness, as you inhale. Fill her with love and compassion as you exhale. Get in touch with that same part of compassion and love that you have when you are concerned about your husband, only this time feel it for that little girl inside you."

About ten minutes later, Laura told me she had succeeded in doing that. I kept reminding her to stay focused on the child and, when her thoughts wandered, to gently bring them back. Finally, the little girl inside Laura started crying. The adult Laura was able to hold her with compassion and suffuse her with love until the child fell asleep in her arms.

I suggested to Laura that she let herself feel the pleasure of peacefulness in her own sleeping inner child and the joy of loving her in this peaceful state. Laura admitted that she felt a strong sense of peace after this experience.

It was probably the first time in Laura's life that she did not have to entertain someone in order to take care of them. She was the oldest of seven children. Her father was an alcoholic. Her mother, who was psychologically and physically absorbed by her husband's disease, had little time for any of the children.

Whenever Laura had painful feelings as a young child, she would escape into the woods behind her house and make up stories to entertain herself. When she reached her teens, she turned to *alcohol and drugs whenever she began to have painful or difficult feelings. Since she was quite attractive, men were easily drawn to her. She lived in a sequence of romantic attachments to handsome, strong men who were unable to feel or express emotions. Unconsciously leaning upon what she had learned from her parents' unbalanced relationship, she knew instinctively that these men felt helpless and loved it when she took care of them and pampered them, even when they were abusive toward her.*

Unfortunately, Laura was re-creating the emotional distance and abuse of her childhood into her adult life. She repeatedly fell in love with men who could help her do this. Laura's task in therapy was to meticulously get in touch with the feelings in her body - the emotions of her inner self - and learn how to take care of herself effectively. Once she accomplished this, it would be safe and possible for her to have a truly loving relationship with an appropriate, non-abusive man.

ROMANCE AND MARRIAGE

If you have a tremendous urge to be in a romantic relationship, and this craving is painful or a major preoccupation in your life, it makes it impossible to keep love going in a long-term relationship – unless you bring the quality of romance back home. Let's find out how to do that now!

Nothing quite matches the high of a new romance. The world is magically transformed into a glittering showcase where all things are possible. Every wish comes true – true in your excited daydreams about the wonderful life you will have together. There is no equal to the glorious anticipation of being with that new, ideal person you fall in love with. The enchantment of being with your lover cures all of your troubles. Finally, the love song and dance is yours!

Why does it feel so good? Because your body, your mind, and your soul are all infused with love. A deeply spiritual person feels the same thing for God. With that kind of loving energy coursing through your veins, you literally can do things you didn't even think of doing before – even smile at that grumpy neighbor across the street.

Why Doesn't Romeo End Up with Juliet?

Most love stories are rife with tragedy. That's because nothing is permanent – you can't hold on to romance as if it were fixed in time and space. The reality of family and other relationship problems always gets in the way of the star-crossed lovers. The biggest reason is that romance is based in large part on delusion – you turned that person you were attracted to into a dream character who possesses all the qualities you longed for. Then comes the crash – the real person who is your lover or your spouse is covered with moles!

Filled with disappointment and anger – if you are a romance addict – you leave and go off in search of a new high. The good news is that it doesn't have to be like this. You are capable of loving – you don't have to search for someone new to have a romantic fix or settle for reading about it in a book. You don't even have to give up your addiction to romance. You will learn in the last part of this chapter how to harvest the elements of romance and use them to breathe new life into your relationship.

True Love versus Romantic Love

True love is unconditional – warts and all. It involves deep devotion to the wellbeing of your lover in good times and bad. You are fully present with them in the moment. Free of judgment and temptations, it is a deeper and broader feeling that goes beyond words. Real love provides solid ground for a romance to flower over and over again. *Romantic love is a flower that wilts quickly if it isn't embedded in real love.*

HARVESTING ROMANTIC QUALITIES

Bring at least one of these qualities into your relationship each day. If you manage to bring them all in, you'll be in what some might call heaven.

Mystery

Discovering new facets about that person you have fallen in love with is intriguing. Never take your partner for granted. Don't think of them in terms of being a fixed item based on an image you have created of them out of your past experiences. We are all changing – all the time. Your mate has vast potentials that seemingly emerge out of nowhere. As changes occur in your mate, allow reciprocal changes to occur in you. Your enthusiasm for each other's growth revitalizes the spirit of romance.

Adventure

Do something new together that you may have been hesitant to do before. One couple I know saves all their money to go to exotic places. Another learned to tango. Yet another couple got turned on by taking Russian lessons together and whispering sweet nothings to each other in that language in bed.

Dreams

You are never too old to dream. Be excited about each other's dreams and help bring them to fruition. Be happy in the process of getting there – that means enjoying each other in the present moment, not waiting for the dream to come true.

Charm

Practice verbalizing the positive things in your life in an excited way and complimenting your partner in life supportively. Do it enthusiastically, from your heart, and romance will flourish. You will have learned to be a charming person. Focus on problems as a challenge rather than as a dead end.

Novelty

While predictability is comforting, it isn't romantic. Try expressing yourself in a novel way or doing something you haven't done before. A French accent in bed might do wonders!

Amorousness

Remember the precious gift of their life that your husband or wife has pledged to you. Express your loving appreciation with tenderness and caring. Now add passion. Keep the enthusiasm of your ardor fresh.

Idyllic Vision

This quality adds depth and intrigue to your vision of your relationship. Your enthusiasm to keep growing is enhanced as your trust for each other expands. You can approach an idyllic state in your relationship but you can't expect it to occur or be sad or angry if it is not already there. It will grow naturally out of love.

Extravagance

Don't hold back in your generosity. Portia was an artist who lived in a small frame house. Anthony, her husband of 40 years, loved collecting tools and stored them in the garage. In an act of generosity, he worked overtime to convert the garage into a beautiful studio and built a shed for his tools. Portia couldn't have been more deeply touched and grateful. Be extravagant in your praise and your expression of love. Be generous with your time and love and in respecting your lover's time and space, even though it means restricting your own different decisions.

Bring it Home

When you see a romantic movie, read a romantic story, or have a romantic memory, find a way to bring it home instead of longing for it. Feel the excitement of creating it with the person you are with. Home is more than a dull place to be comfortable. Make it an incubator for romance that never dies. Sing that love song in your voice, now! You don't have to have a good voice to *be* the song. All you have to do is feel it from your heart and let it flow.

Magnifying the Pleasure

When something pleasant happens between you and your partner, enjoy recounting what you liked about it. Celebrate your harmonious experiences with a toast to each other.

Sex

When you bring romance back into your marriage, your excitement will naturally get your hormones flowing. Think of all the ways you can introduce these different facets into your sex life. **Have fun with it!** And now that we've brought up the subject, let's talk some more about it in the next chapter.

THE ZEN OF
SEXUALITY

The Zen of sexuality offers a uniquely satisfying approach to the ages-old fascination with human sexuality. I wrote the following poem to illustrate Zen's power to transform one of our most powerful instincts. The words and rhythm of this poem are, indeed, designed to describe the Zen of sexuality in action:

NAKED BEFORE YOU

Love emerging
Here I am, bare and vulnerable
Fully exposed to the one I love
Eyes caring tenderly
An invitation to share
Devotion to comfort and pleasure I can give
Free of concerns of myself
Spirit and flesh, pulsing, pulsing back and forth
Bodies anointed in the warmth of devotion
The tingling energy of love blossoms in ritual fulness
Lips, hands, ecstatic in the exquisite dance of giving
and receiving. Moving as they touch,
from tenderness to passion.
Seeking acceptance and reaching that which is precious
Bodies merging in the spices of taste and smell
All cells, even those held most private, join in the
Ecstasy of togetherness. Inter-being,
no you, no me, only we,
we who are one.
No thought of looking, no thought of touching,

no thought of taste or smell
I am my vision, I am my touch, I am my taste and smell.
I am far more, I am love
Love that has no beginning and no end.
Love that is everything and no "thing" at the same time.
Love that is interdependent co-arising
with each racing heartbeat

All the statues of the Buddha show him sitting in marvelous repose, peacefully contemplating. He has a slight smile on his face. I am moved to think he would give us a mischievous wink as we go through this chapter together.

Following the principles Buddha discovered thousands of years ago will do wonders for your sex life. It involves giving up concepts and judgments about sex that have conditioned us to respond in limited ways. These concepts have been handed down for generations directly from our parents to us and are promulgated everywhere we turn through the media. In fact, a Zen approach to sexuality involves giving up all thought and being there totally, in loving, intensely sensual bliss. The first part of the chapter explains how we can do that on a moment-to-moment basis. The second part offers solutions for past experiences that can inhibit us or make us afraid, hampering our ability to enjoy the Zen of sexuality. The guiding principles to success here are simple and effective in their goals:

1 Always touch your mate with loving enthusiasm and admiration for the special person they are.
2 Never do anything that is hurtful to the one you love.

DESIRE CAN GROW OR
DESTROY LOVE

When your desire stems from the fulness of love coursing urgently through your body as physical sensations, the excitement of wanting to share this with the special
person next to you is desire that grows love and is truly a gift
from God. If, on the other hand, your desire stems from a
sense of emptiness inside, you end up thinking of yourself as
a little thing that has to have that sexy person over there to be
whole. Your desire destroys love when you crave attachment
to the other person. Desire then becomes painful. If it is not
fulfilled you feel hurt, angry, and disappointed. Total fulfillment is impossible. You may feel brief satisfaction, but you
end up being consumed by the fires of disappointment
because ultimately **you can only use your sexuality to express
love, not to extract it.** Desire laced with devotion - where
your happiness is in terms of what you can do for your lover
- is the way to freedom and fulfillment. You're not using
your partner to feel good about yourself – you're touching
them to express the beauty that is already within you.

HOW TO TRANSFORM DESIRE INTO LOVING ENTHUSIASM

You become aware of your thoughts about that body lying next to you. Because of your preconditioned concepts, it has a special shape and form you label either as sexy and want to possess, or unattractive and want to avoid. This creates the pain of disappointment and anger if the person who owns that body rejects being possessed by you or you reject them. The key to freedom here is to **be aware of your own thoughts, your own fixed concepts of what is sexy, and let them go.** You do this by paying attention, first of all, to your breathing, as we've discussed before:

❖ Being mindful of my breath brings me into the physical realm of my existence and extricates me from the trap of my own tangled thought processes. My mind is focused on my belly rising as I breathe in and falling as I breathe out.

❖ As my mind quietens I let myself be aware of the energy coursing through my body. The more I give up thoughts about what is going on or about what should be going on, and replace it with simple awareness of my body's energy, the more my sensuality grows.

❖ I don't limit it to my sexual organs. I start by paying attention to the energy vibrating there and gradually let it spread to the rest of my body. I bring each part of my body alive by paying attention to it. Breathing in, I feel the vibrations in my lips, or my hands; breathing out, I experience it growing in a pleasant way. I do the same with my legs, chest, and back – all parts of my body. I breathe loving energy into each part of my body as this process goes on.

✤ I now experience the joy of my fulness and the excitement of wanting to use it to express the totality of love with my lover. As they do the same with me, we become two beings united physically and emotionally in our devotion to each other.

This attitude, as you can imagine, is dramatically different to much of Western society's commodity-driven version of sexuality. It is decidedly not part of the egregious "wham, bam – thank-you ma'am" school of thought.

To Summarize

Ecstasy, the marvelous wonder that small children effortlessly achieve in the act of discovery, is not something you grab or attempt to reach - it is already there. Each touch, each fragrance, each sight is a wonder of this ecstatic moment. The process of watching your thoughts and physical sensations - being intimate with them - frees you of responding in a conditioned or conventional way. You aren't making love to prove you are a man or a woman - love is already there. You are simply and elegantly letting your mind come to a state of quiet, opening your heart to it and enabling your heartfelt devotion to take over your body.

TANTRIC SEXUALITY

About five thousand years ago in India, mystics talked about the spiritual union of body and mind, exemplified in the highest form of sexual union. They have developed many meditations and physical exercises that help lovers experience this divine union. In *The Art of Sexual Ecstasy*, Margot Anand provides a modernized program with specific exercises that teach Tantric sex, enabling anyone to incorporate sexuality and spirituality into their daily lives.

IMPOTENCE AND FRIGIDITY –
TRUTH MACHINES

Instead of being frightened or frustrated by impotence or frigidity, treat it as you would a red light. Stop, look inside, and see what's going on. First, check with your physician to rule out any physical problems that may be present. Once these have been addressed, look into the emotional health of your relationship. Being the most sensitive, tender, and personal parts of your body, your sexual organs speak eloquently either of love or problems. What problems are present? What impasses keep love from flowing freely? Simply reading the list of topics in the table of contents at the front of this book may bring the hidden obstacle to conscious awareness. Then you can deal with it in a compassionate, caring manner. Are you closing down because of script rules from childhood or emotional scars from old sexual traumas? Is there some problem that is distancing you emotionally from your lover? Instead of being critical of the truth machine, welcome it as an opportunity to deepen your relationship.

SEX AFTER SIXTY, SEVENTY, EIGHTY, OR NINETY-TWO

The beauty of aging is that it invites you to slow down. The way you express yourself as you get older may be very different from when you were a teenager. Slowing down enables the passion to be deeper, more prolonged, and more meaningful. Instead of rushing towards an end, each precious moment is enjoyed in the here and now, knowing that there may not be a tomorrow. The comfort of touch and self-acceptance that comes with commitment – based not on appearances but on love - affords marvelous security for letting sex in any form play its way out.

"FREE" SEX

When people talk about "free sex" they are usually referring to having intercourse with anyone they are attracted to, with no strings attached, abandoning themselves to the pleasure of the moment. Unfortunately, there is nothing free about it – the most personal parts of your body are being bartered for momentary pleasure. This discounts the preciousness of the only vehicle you possess to express your aliveness. If either one of the pair engaging in such activity has caring feelings, the emotional pain of being used is very costly. Then there is the emotional toll paid to our other fears such as disease, pregnancy, anxiety, and physical rejection that go with having sex with strangers or casual acquaintances. There is no such thing as free sex in a relationship devoid of love.

Free Sex in a Committed Relationship

When your commitment to love each other is unconditional, you are free to express your sensuality in ways that are not harmful to your lover. The greater your commitment to love, the freer you can be in bed. You can give up concepts of he, she, and how it is to be and experience passion at its best. There are no forbidden acts because there is no judgment – only the desire to share the fulness of your devotion to each other.

This is the essence of the Zen of sexuality – mindfulness of the body expressing love in action, broader and deeper than thought.

SEX – PATHWAY TO LOVE OR DEAD END TO DESPAIR

In a new relationship, the joy of sharing your body can lead to momentary loving appreciation of your partner for the pleasure they have shared. It can serve as an introduction to intimacy. But sex can also be used to avoid intimacy. This occurs in a person who is addicted to sex.

CASE VIGNETTE:
ADDICTION TO SEX

Jerome, *a prominent lawyer in his thirties, was devoted to his wife and five-year-old son. He had a roving eye but didn't stray until both of his parents were killed in a crash. Jerome was shocked by his loss but maintained his touch as a prosecuting attorney until after the funeral. Shortly after that, he found a mistress. Anytime he felt the slightest bit down, he went to her for sex. He became obsessed with her faithfulness to him. Flashing a lot of money landed him a second mistress. When he came to see me, he was frantic with the fear that he would lose his wife who by then had become aware of his cheating.*

He didn't feel capable of giving up his mistresses – "They bring me the only excitement I have," he told me – but through therapy he was finally able to come to terms with his grief. He was able to comfort the five-year-old Jerome inside of him who was terrified of abandonment. It had been too risky emotionally to go to his wife for nurturing. (He said at one point, "She is the only person left in the world who loves me. If she rejects me, I'll kill myself.") As is the case with any addiction, sex can be used to avoid pain or to seek momentary pleasure when there is no real joy in life. Jerome reported that he had no emotional ties with his mistresses – he just enjoyed his sense of power in "turning them on." It was a frantic attempt to feel strong and avoid the vulnerability of his intense need to be taken care of.

When he learned how to love his inner self with the help of his understanding wife, he gave up his addiction and learned how to cherish being with his family.

MEN IN HIGH PLACES

A ddiction to sex is common among political and corporate executives who have tremendous responsibilities,
disposable income, power, and the means to exercise it. They
also have to present an image to themselves and the outside
world of strength and invulnerability. They often believe
they can't go to their wives and admit vulnerability or fear.
The physical content of their sexual adventures, as it was
with Jerome, is an attempt at closeness that reinforces their
sense of power, but obscures intimacy with themselves and
others. This leads to a sense of emptiness and longing that is
never fulfilled. It can contribute to an unquenchable com-
pensatory thirst for power.

SUMMARY

I n this chapter, we discussed how sex can become a vehicle
for deep communion, or used in a manner that destroys
intimacy. As one approaches mid-life (our first call to eterni-
ty), the temptation is great to cling to sexuality in a vain
attempt to hold on to youthfulness and ward off the shadows
of aging. Staying intimate with your life partner, as the next
chapter will help you do, will enable you to sail through this
difficult period. You can be a much better person than you
ever thought possible.

MID-LIFE
CRISIS

FIRST CALL TO ETERNITY

M id-life is a time when many people go through the futile attempt to change their fate by changing their mate. This chapter will show you how to embrace middle age as an optimum time of life in which you retain your energy and have the wisdom to use it wisely. It is a time that calls for change – an internal change that makes life more meaningful and deepens your joy of being alive. It is a time for life partners to inspire each other. This chapter will make it easier to do that by helping you identify underlying fears and transforming them into opportunities for refreshing yourself and your relationship.

Time immemorial in all its richness is present in this moment. Facing it upright, without leaning back into the past or racing on to the future, incorporates the splendor of all that is. Mid-life offers us a wonderful opportunity to experience that reality.

THE RACE TO NOWHERE

T he good news about fear is that it disappears if you face it squarely and nurture yourself through it. The bad news is that it can grow into terror if you run away from it. Our culture's addiction to youthfulness represents a mass attempt at escape from the fear of aging by focusing on sexual attractiveness. This adds to the difficulty men and women have accepting each other as they are. It turns the sexes into cartoon characters who are always chasing each other, frequently colliding but not often meeting.

A man who sees his hairline receding and his temples graying can no longer fit himself into an image of youthfulness. He hunts for an attractive younger woman to look at. Scanning her beauty keeps him from looking at his own face, scowling at his aging image. A woman, meanwhile, spends a fortune in time, lotions, and surgery trying to stay attractive; capturing a man's attention provides a magical escape from the wrinkles for a while.

The race away from aging can take any path – too much exercise, a shiny new sports car, an obsession with money or clothes, overly protective parenting. People cling to an endless variety of activities to avoid thinking that they are getting older. Examine the way you spend your time. You can identify escapist activity by the compulsive, urgent "do or die" tension associated with it. You keep chasing your goal no matter how detrimental it is to the rest of your life.

How to Stop the Race

There is no easy answer here, but this procedure can help:

✤ Gently but firmly stop whatever you are doing that has a compulsive edge to it.
✤ Let yourself feel the agitation and anxiety that occurs when you stop.
✤ Use the Inner Self Meditation outlined in Chapter 2 to relieve anxiety. Now you are ready to find some answers to the fears underlying your mid-life crisis.

The following case vignette is an illustration of the fear many people are partially aware of – "I won't be able to enjoy myself in the same way I did (or fantasized doing) before." The more profound apprehensions – "I'm wasting my life" or "I'm afraid of dying" are pushed further out of conscious awareness.

CASE VIGNETTE:
THE MAN WHO HAD IT ALL

M*artin had a beautiful wife who loved him, two children he adored, a highly successful business, and more money than he could spend in a lifetime. He was also miserable.*

As Martin approached 40, he was terrified of becoming the workaholic his father was – an unhappy, driven man, stuck in an unhappy marriage. Martin saw nothing but drudgery and over-whelming responsibilities in his future. His wife, Mary, was a worrier who took everything so seriously she wasn't fun to be around. Still, Martin couldn't stand the thought of living away from his children and inflicting the pain on them that he had experienced as a child when his parents separated.

He was in a typical mid-life crisis. Forty marked a downhill path in which his natural buoyant spirit would be suffocated by responsibilities. He feared he was becoming more like Mary, whom he never felt enjoyed herself because she was so busy "doing the right thing."

Martin fell in love with Margie, a beautiful 26-year-old who, to him "epitomized the idea of youthful freedom," as he would describe it. Mostly, he said, he enjoyed laughing with her. She had a great sense of humor which supported his own. He dreamed of divorcing Mary, but he couldn't. Because of his crush on Margie, it took 12 months of therapy to help him discover that the ability to enjoy life was a skill of his own making. He didn't have to attach himself to Margie to experience it.

He understood that he had put Mary in a rigid frame, not only in his own mind but also on a practical level. He had ceded the role of the children's disciplinarian to Mary. He learned to take over this role himself in a manner that was light-hearted but effective. This freed Mary to be more spontaneous and fun to be around. Over a period of time, Martin succeeded in bringing the attributes he enjoyed in his relationship with Margie into his own marriage. He learned he didn't have to cling to old ways of enjoying himself and no longer feared "getting too old to live."

JOY

M any people in our culture associate having a good time with drinking and using drugs. As they mature, they see the drawbacks of "partying" and sense the futility of trying to be happy through the use of so-called "recreational chemicals." At the same time, they fear growing older and giving up that old way of enjoying themselves.

What you enjoy has more to do with what you are thinking and feeling than what you are doing. The pursuit of joy keeps you from enjoying this moment – the only moment we have. Watch any toddler who has received enough love and attention and you'll immediately see what I mean. Those toddlers can, in fact, show you precisely how to experience joy.

They come smiling to the outside world with the creativity of an artist, the inquisitiveness of a scientist, and the free spontaneity of someone who gives and takes warmth freely. Any adult who can do that without becoming drunk first is a much sought-after person who is never lonely. When you learn how to do this, you won't have to leave home to have a good time.

Contrast the toddler's ebullient spontaneity with the internal dialogue of a patient named Rochelle. Her internal dialogue when she attends a party goes something like this: "Pull in your stomach. Your outfit is too tight and too dressy. Smile and look interested. You should remember everyone's name. Don't bore people – think of something clever to say. Stop fidgeting. Why are you such a wimp? There's nothing to be afraid of. Have another drink – lighten up!"

Imagine 15 people at that same party with a similar dialogue and you can understand why everyone is walking around clutching a drink. The same alcohol that quiets the self-criticism can also wipe out one's conscientious concern about a partner, and often turns otherwise playful flirting into marriage-disrupting seduction.

HOW TO GET A NATURAL HIGH

That charming toddler is still alive in you. You can revive its bouncy spontaneity and add some spice of adult sophistication by doing the same things that drugs and alcohol do: silence self-criticism and stimulate your brain's pleasure centers. The following exercise can enable you to accomplish this minor miracle.

A "GO WITH IT" EXERCISE

+ *If you're anxious, do the Inner Self Meditation you learned in Chapter 2 until you feel comfortable. With practice, it takes less than a minute.*

+ *Smile at the memory of some episode in the past when you felt joy and/or were loved by someone. Breathe the emotions in and let yourself feel them now.*

+ *In your mind's eye, imagine what it would be like to experience those positive emotions now as you meet someone for the first time or take part in some new activity.*

+ *If you feel your body tensing up, if you feel nervous or anxious, understand that the feeling is a response to self-criticism creeping in. Respond by changing your attitude to one that encourages your inner child to "go with it." It might even be helpful for your adult self to say something like, "Go with it, kid — I'm here for you no matter what happens."*

In my practice, I've often seen this technique work with very little effort. Most patients feel a spontaneous impulse to do or say something that is, for them, a creative change from their past patterns of behavior in such situations. The bottom line is simple: As long as it isn't harmful to you or someone else, do it!

I know this might not sound so spontaneous, but practicing the "go with it" technique reprograms you to be comfortable with spontaneity. Then you don't have to cling to old ways of having fun. You can bring the freshness of a toddler's joy to all areas of your life, including your relationship.

A BLESSING DRESSED IN FEAR'S CLOTHING

There is one fear of middle age that needs to be treated with great reverence. It serves as a spiritual danger signal that you are not spending your precious life energy in a manner that is congruent with your highest intentions.

Your body is filled with a vibrant, internal energy that is on loan to you for the duration of your life. Are you spending your days growing in your ability to love? Are you enjoying what you do and getting better at it? Are you in some small way making the world a better place? Or, are you passing your days routinely doing what you have to do, waiting for something – or someone – better to come your way? Your mid-life crisis is a crisis of decision. Will you arrange the last half of your life so that it unfolds in a manner that is meaningful for you and others around you?

Make believe that you are 95 and you are looking back on your life. What would you have done differently with your friends and loved ones? How would you have changed your profession? What would you have done more, or less of, in your everyday life?

Talk over all of this with your partner and make a list of things you would like to change. Loving each other through the adventure of change will restore the edge to your relationship. You are embarking on a romance with life that partnering makes easier and more exciting. It can – and often does – restore your togetherness.

FEAR OF DEATH

Acknowledging that your life is half over brings the shadow of death halfway closer. This aspect of aging is usually pushed far out of awareness by the frantic drive to do everything "before it's too late." One patient said recently, "I have no time to live." He ran his own business but it left no time in the busy schedule he had created for the things he enjoyed – making love to his wife, relaxing, exercising. He was genuinely surprised to notice that his hair had turned gray.

Death as an Illumination of Life

It is best to accept death as another part of your life experience. Don't yearn for its peacefulness and don't run away from it. Use the awareness of death to highlight the preciousness of each moment of life.

ILLUMINATION OF LIFE MEDITATION

✤ *Let thoughts pass by you as you shift your focus to your heart.*
  Breathe in and out of your heart.

✤ *Remember a time you felt love for anyone (a pet will do fine).*

✤ *Experience the love as an energy force you are inhaling into*
  your heart. As you exhale, send the love back out to the uni-
  verse. Enjoy reinforcing your loving feelings by visualizing
  the force becoming brighter with exhalation.

✤ *Enjoy the experience of your heart being a powerful genera-*
  tor of love for a few minutes.

✤ *Be aware of the preciousness of this moment in the light of*
  love.

✤ *This moment has no beginning and no end. It is always there*
  for you to enjoy.

✤ *Staying fully in this moment without clinging to the past or*
  worrying about the future is the antidote to the fear of dying.

Death and Relationships

As we discussed in Chapter 4, many people avoid closeness
because of the fear of losing the one they love. Be aware of
that fear and use your heart to intensify your love for that
person in this second. The "Hugging Meditation" introduced by Thich Nhat Hanh a prominent Buddhist teacher,
illustrates this beautifully:

HUGGING MEDITATION

❖ *Hold someone you care for closely.*

❖ *Breathe in and out three times. Each time you inhale, take in their love, and each time you exhale, send them your love.*

❖ *Step apart for a moment. Remind yourself that either of you may die at any time.*

❖ *Hug that person again. With your renewed awareness, feel the preciousness of this person as you share your love at a deeper level.*

SUMMARY

Middle age presents you with a crossroad in life filled with opportunity. You can harvest the best parts of your youth and hone it with the wisdom of experience. Antidotes to the fear of aging were discussed which you can use to:

❖ Deepen joyful experiences

❖ Change your focus to bring more fulfilling meaning to your life

❖ Profoundly appreciate the preciousness of each moment and those you love.

THE SEVEN
YEAR ITCH –
FINDING FUN
IN FIDELITY

TOO HOT TO HANDLE

You are alone and blue, wondering what to do with yourself. Your wife and two kids left town for a month's vacation early that morning and you're looking forward to their first phone call.

Suddenly, you hear a creaking noise in the ceiling. You thought the trapdoor leading to the upstairs apartment was locked, but it slowly opens and the face of an astonishingly beautiful woman appears. Her smile sends delicious shivers down your spine and she asks permission to join you. You try to sound casual as you offer her coffee, but you can't control your eyes – they're glued to her impossibly beautiful body. This is all too good to be true. It feels like a dream but you couldn't possibly dream up the scent of her perfume. She seems to like you, which sends your mind reeling with fantasies of what can happen in the month ahead.

Then the phone rings. You're flooded with guilt when you hear the warmth in your wife's voice and the excited stories of the children. The anticipated pleasure of hearing from them has turned into a nightmare of conflicting emotions in ten minutes, and all you have done is offer a neighbor a cup of coffee.

Movie fans probably recognize this sequence of events from the Marilyn Monroe classic, *The Seven Year Itch*. In this Hollywood version, our hero – played by the sad sack comic actor, Tom Ewell – struggles valiantly with temptation and the story ultimately has a happy ending for everyone. Your personal version of this theme can unfold at any time for you or your loved one. Temptations are everywhere and something like the "Seven Year Itch" could happen at any time – from your honeymoon to even your golden wedding anniversary.

NO MATTER HOW MUCH IT ITCHES – DON'T SCRATCH!

If you or your mate develops a yearning to be with someone else, don't panic! It doesn't mean your relationship is on the rocks or that you are a bad person. It does mean, however, that some important needs within yourself or the relationship aren't being fulfilled. This chapter will help you identify them and empower you to create your own happy ending. To accomplish this, it is important that the itch to try someone new remains at the fantasy level. Daydreams are important and can be useful, but scratching the itch can infect your whole life.

Beware of the Titanic – *A Visit to Dreamland*

But you might say to yourself, "I owe it to myself to get to know this dreamboat that has come into my life. I've always dreamed of being with someone just like this and they seem interested in me. I can't believe they're interested in me! I can't pass up this chance of a lifetime. It wouldn't hurt to have an innocent cup of coffee together."

Affairs, like other romantic beginnings, often have a dreamlike quality. The elements of secrecy and the lure of forbidden fruit create added excitement that comes from courting danger. You are the romantic lead in your own movie, but the danger comes from losing yourself in the role. Hidden from the real world in a secluded setting, you are ignited with excitement and enraptured by the promise of pleasure this new person seems to embody.

At home after your brief encounter, you will likely feel alienated from your family. You may feel not fully "there." You may long to be back in your dream world because home may come to represent the drudgery of everyday life, with unresolved conflicts and decisions to be made. Your family, meanwhile, senses your subtle withdrawal and retreats into a safe nucleus, which leaves you feeling even more alienated. Feeling alone, you miss your new "love." You lament, "My partner never makes me feel this way." The new person feels even more special to you.

Of course, both you and your intended lover are at your polished best during your brief encounters. As time goes by, however, you slowly reveal your true selves to each other. The relationship may cool and the resulting icebergs you run into elsewhere in your life can turn your dreamboat into a personal *Titanic*.

A TRAP CALLED DESIRE

Imagine resting comfortably on a beautiful beach. The warm sun and cool breezes soothe your skin. The gentle surf quiets your heart. All is well – you are cloaked in a wonderful sense of peace.

A man and a woman walk by, holding hands. You fill your mind with an imagined story about their happiness. Suddenly, a heavy cloud of misery darkens your heart. You have no one to play the romantic lead opposite you in your own life story! The conflicting pain of longing for someone new, and the misery accompanying the thought of giving up what you already have, can drown you in waves of loneliness. The beach, an island of contentment a few minutes ago, has instead become an expansive prison of unbearable isolation.

How did that happen? Your sense of wellbeing is painfully destroyed when your mind attaches itself to a desire for someone or something outside of yourself. *As you focus your attention and energy on getting, you are giving up being.*

Avoiding the Trap

All you have to remember, however, is that true inner peace and freedom come from recognizing and nurturing that which is already within you. You don't have to look for it elsewhere. The security that comes with being part of a couple lovingly committed to each other permits freedom to expand exponentially. The arena of trust you have created makes it less risky for you to explore and nurture new facets of yourself and each other that may be lying dormant. Supporting new growth in each other is the exciting stuff that creates soul mates. This is the ultimate romance we'll be talking about in the final chapter.

POTHOLES IN MARRIAGE

L et's talk about how to avoid some of the major potholes in marriage and long-term relationships that damage intimacy and can propel you into an affair or divorce.

Anger – A Weed in the Garden of Your Mind

Think of your unconscious mind as a garden with seeds of love, peace, anger, sadness, fear, and other emotions. Each time you have an emotion, you water its seeds and it occupies more space. When you water the seed of anger, it strangles positive emotions. In the future, anger is more and more liable to pop up in your conscious mind. It becomes a habit that destroys intimacy.

What to Do with Your Anger

We used to advise couples to express anger to each other whenever they felt it. We exhorted them to "Get it off your chest!" We were wrong. Yes, it is important to recognize that you are angry and respect it. It is always justifiable to some part of your personality, and is a valuable emotion that signals frustration, hurt, and danger. Don't bury it but don't use it against your mate because it suffocates love and promotes conflict.

Disagreements that generate anger are unavoidable even in the best relationships. In fact, the closer you become to someone, the more your differences can provoke anger. Our challenge is to transform it into a balm that heals the pain of disagreement.

Disagreement – A Blessing in Disguise

As infants we need to be cuddled. Without touch, we become very ill and can die. Our existence needs to be validated by loving touch. As adults, the identity we have constructed as the result of our life experiences (conditioning) requires respect and loving confirmation. We are very attached to the beliefs and standards associated with that self-image. When our mate's behavior or ideas conflict with our own, it is especially threatening to our self-esteem. We feel hurt or angry. "How," we may ask ourselves, "can the person I love be so inconsiderate or have so little understanding?" This often takes the form of an admonition such as, "If you really loved me, you would _____" (At this point, feel free to take a few minutes to fill in the space.)

Since no two of us have identical life experiences, we don't feel, think, or act alike. Growth and intimacy at a deeper level come through the resolution of disagreements. In order to really open our hearts to our loved ones, we have to give up being so attached to our own beliefs of right or wrong and put ourselves in each other's shoes. This brings us closer to the reality that we are more than our thoughts, more than our bodies, more than our feelings. We have a higher self that is one with God – a self that is understanding and loving. When the higher selves of you and your mate connect, you are on the way to being soul mates. (More on this in the final chapter.)

How to Transform Anger

To solve disagreements, we have to transform anger into compassion and understanding that heals. Here is the way to achieve that goal: start by signing an anger contract.

> ### ANGER CONTRACT
>
> *Write and sign an anger contract that reads something like this: "I agree that when either of us is angry we will avoid arguing. I will inform you that what you did or didn't do hurt me and I feel angry. We agree not to talk about it until (set a definite time and day) when we can resolve this disagreement peacefully. Until that time, I will take care of my anger by transforming it into understanding. I will put myself into your shoes to really be with you in your feelings."*

Here are three ways to transform anger – use the one that works best for you.*

---

* This is an adaptation from *Freeze Frame*, developed by Dr Lew Childre (Planetary Publications, 1994)

I. MOVE FROM YOUR HEAD TO YOUR HEART

1 *Recognize that you are angry and stop yourself from expressing it verbally or physically. Give yourself a break from the painful interchange.*

2 *Move your attention away from your head, which is full of thoughts justifying your anger, to your heart, which has a well-developed nervous system that can lead you to a solution based on wisdom and love.*

3 *Recall any positive experience in which you are loving someone or just having fun. Imagine you are in that experience right now. Imagine you are not imaging – you really are having that experience right now.*

4 *Breathe in the positive energy of the memory you are reliving into your heart. You might feel the warmth of the energy or see it as shimmering light. As you exhale, sense it flowing out of your heart into your bloodstream to all parts of your body. Continue doing this as the tug to return your attention to the turbulence oin your head diminishes in intensity.*

5 *As your heart to help you use your intuitive and caring self to come up with a response to the situation which would cause the least amount of disharmony now and in the future.*

As you breathe in and out of your heart, don't try to think of an answer – let it drift out of your heart. It may come in the form of a daydream. Don't be concerned if your heart doesn't immediately give you an answer. Just employing the technique will reduce the intensity of your anger.

2. MEDITATION ON THE INNER SELF

1 *Remember having loving feelings toward someone or something (a pet will do fine).*

2 *Focus on that loving feeling and imagine breathing it into every cell of your body. Fill yourself with loving energy.*

3 *Locate where in your body the feeling of anger is centered. Common places are the heart, stomach, or throat – but it can be anywhere. It may even be sensed by your whole body.*

4 *Imagine seeing, hearing, touching the angry part of yourself. You might "see" an angry expression on the image of that part of you, or it might appear as a vague sensation. That part may be any age, from infancy up to your present age.*

5 *Imagine holding that angry part of you tenderly in your arms. Take a deep breath and visualize that you are breathing in the angry feelings. Your outer self is now being a perfect mother or father, being mindful of – and totally accepting of – the anger in your inner self.*

6 *As you breathe out, be aware that you are exhaling feelings of love and compassion to your inner self. Send that loving energy out with all your heart.*

7 *Keep focused. Forget the circumstances or the cause of the anger at the time. Your inner self needs your total care and attention. Simply keep breathing in the dark energy of anger and sending back the lighter energy of love and compassion. You are using your body, mind, and soul to transform anger into love. Keep doing this until you notice a change. The anger might change into another emotion – sadness, for*

example. Continue breathing in the new emotion, accepting it totally and sending love and compassion to your inner self. Continue until you feel relief. This usually occurs in a few minutes if you stay focused. If your mind wanders, it requires more time. If you have difficulty identifying specific emotions, imagine breathing in a dark, heavy energy and breathing out to the inner self a lighter white energy.

3. MEDITATION ON ANGER

1 *Breathe deep down into your abdomen. Count up to ten breaths and repeat the count. Watch your abdomen rise as you breathe in and fall as you breathe out.*

2 *Notice your mind racing and gently bring it back to your breathing.*

3 *Don't try to stop your thoughts. Simply be aware of them, let them pass, and return to your breathing.*

4 *You can say to yourself, "Breathing in, I'm aware I am angry – breathing out, I'm aware I am angry." Just watch the emotion increase or decrease in intensity.*

5 *Be empathetic and non-critical of your anger like a mother soothing a small baby.*

6 *You may notice thoughts coming up that generate new anger. Don't attach to them. Let them go and return to your breathing. Your anger will gradually disappear.*

"You Don't Make Me Happy"

You are depressed about your job and look over at your partner watching television. Your sadness turns to anger when the thought crosses your mind that he or she "never does anything to make me happy."

It is important that you never look to another person to make you happy. Happiness is an internal experience that no one else can create for you. You have that good feeling naturally when you are at peace with yourself and use your life energy to share the physical, intellectual, emotional, and spiritual parts of yourself in a caring way. When you do that, you feel powerful and independent. You are whole as you are. You don't have to search for someone else to make you complete.

If you have been expecting your mate to make you happy, you end up angry and disappointed. You find fault with them and use this as an excuse to get lost in your children, your career, or something else to "make you happy."

Emotional pain comes when you fail to use your life energy to live fully in the present moment and long for something or someone else to fulfill this moment for you. This happens when:

✤ You have unrealistic expectations for yourself
✤ You are self-critical
✤ You cling to the past and/or are fearful of the future.

On those occasions, you are not enjoying your own power. You become vulnerable by attaching yourself to other people to use their power.

Albert and Tina's story provides hints about what can happen when people expect others to make them happy.

CASE VIGNETTE:
AN INTERNET AFFAIR

A lbert is a very successful physician. His wife, Tina, is a devoted homemaker and mother of their three children. They both do their jobs well – they even enjoy sex with each other. But they barely talk about anything that isn't related to family.

Albert is bored with Tina and joins an internet chat line where he meets Renée. Soon, he is spending more and more time on-line with Renée – a brilliant correspondent who both challenges and supports his political and spiritual ideals. Their intellectual chats become spiced with sexual innuendoes. They exchange photographs. Renée, Albert discovers, is not only smart but beautiful too, and he falls in love with his fantasies about her. Even though he is torn by guilt, he makes plans to rendezvous with her. At that point, Albert comes to see me professionally.

Albert quickly realizes that as long as Renée was an anonymous figure on the internet, there was no risk in expressing himself freely. He decided that Tina and his family were what he treasured most in his life and gave up plans to meet Renée. Meanwhile, he began talking to Tina in the same way he did with Renée and was overjoyed to discover how responsive she was. Tina had buried her intellectual side when she became a homemaker and soon blossomed at the opportunity to have adult conversations with Albert. He was even more delighted when "talking dirty" to Tina in bed turned her on.

Boredom – Clinging to Past Pleasures

That first taste of whipped cream is sweet and smooth on your tongue. "Delicious," you tell yourself, "I want more!" As you eat more of it, your taste buds become exhausted and you eventually react indifferently. But if you continue to eat it, you may feel nauseated and disgusted with yourself. The same thing happens when otherwise good relationships remain unchanged.

What first charmed you about your mate may now bore you or elicit feelings of contempt. It is important not to cling to past ways of enjoying yourself. If you keep exploring new activities and learning new things, you can avoid growing old inside. When you do this in life with your partner, excitement replaces boredom and your relationship flourishes.

Boredom is a Decision

A child confined to a small space is denied the natural excitement that comes from exploring new vistas. A wise parent brings a wide variety of toys to keep their child from becoming irritated and bored on a long journey. As adults we are responsible for keeping ourselves excited and interested in our surroundings. It is empowering to think of boredom as a decision. In marriage and long-term relationships, we can either decide to be bored by what is, or find excitement by exploring new dimensions of ourselves and our relationship.

The Don'ts of Boredom

✦ If you feel bored, don't blame your spouse or the institution of marriage. Commitment is a dedication to love, not to the limitations of keeping things the same.

✦ Don't look for excitement by having an affair. (In a few moments, you'll discover what to do if you are turned on by some third party.)

✦ Don't expect your mate to provide excitement for you. Excitement has to originate within yourself, then you can share it.

✦ Don't attempt to hold on to old ways of creating romance.

Solutions to Boredom

✦ Do bring romance back into your relationship by exploring new ways of expressing your love. Chapters 7 and 12 provide a good place to start.

✦ Do stop and ask yourself, "What do I want physically at this moment? What do I want emotionally and intellectually?" The answers can change from moment to moment. For example, when I ask myself those questions at this time, I find that I am fatigued intellectually from writing – so I wouldn't be interested right now in additional intellectual challenges. Writing also involves emotional giving; my inner self tells me it's time to take in some caring from outside. Physically, my body is asking for action. A long, brisk walk in the park holding hands with my wife as we take in the beauty of nature would be ideal.

My partner's needs, based on these criteria, may be different. As a loving act I might compromise and do something that fits her needs at this moment. I might go for the walk by myself and meet her later. What I decide has to be a free decision based on loving awareness of my own needs as well as hers. This is love in action. This is never boring. It combines spontaneity and caring with planning. When you add creative imagination to the mix, it sets the stage for a long and lasting romance with life and each other.

Children – A Menace to Marriage

CASE VIGNETTE: JOHNNY

J ohnny, the oldest of five children, told me that his wife, Esther, had been a dream come true for him. For two years, this beautiful woman had adored him. It was thrilling for her to fix his favorite lasagna and even more thrilling to please him in bed. She was excited about his victories at work and nurtured him through disappointment. As a child, Johnny had received little attention from his exhausted mother. Now, for the first time in his life, he was receiving adequate nurturing. In addition, he had a wonderful playmate. But everything changed ten years ago when their son, John Jr., was born.

Esther, on the other hand, was the youngest of four. Her mother was preoccupied with her husband's drinking problem, so the love Esther experienced as a child came as isolated events she could never count on. She was therefore determined to be there for John Jr. Breastfeeding continued for two years – her breasts and the rest of her body were completely devoted to nursing. Sex became an irritating intrusion on her primary focus of being a perfect mother. She didn't trust babysitters, so three years passed before the couple finally went out on another date together.

Johnny, meanwhile, loved his son and enjoyed being with him, but felt painfully restricted by Esther. The adult playmate and doting spouse had disappeared. Instead, she symbolized entrapment to him and he grew resentful. Longing for the good feelings he once had for Esther, he turned to other women.

When I ask couples to date the onset of their difficulties with each other, the most frequent answer is the birth of their first child. The love they had given to each other is poured into the children. This is particularly true of couples who received poor parenting themselves. They strive to be a perfect mother or father in order to shield their child from the emotional deprivations they experienced as children.

The total attention Esther gave to Johnny Jr. is only necessary for a few months and slowly diminishes with each passing month and year. What the child really needs as he or she grows older is the support to be more and more on his own. The security of having a mother and father who love each other is the family safety net. The example they set for having fun together is a template for the child to follow when they enter a committed relationship of their own later in life. It is crucial that devotion to the happiness of each other maintains at least equal importance as the devotion to a child. Loving each other as they share love with the children makes the relationship whole.

SUMMARY

Researchers report that affairs have been occurring with increasing frequency in the past thirty years. An affair, as we learned elsewhere in this book, is a betrayal of trust that destroys intimacy. In the following chapter you will find out what to do when either of you is attracted to someone else. You'll also find your painful longing for an affair will change into fun and excitement with your mate as you discover how to take on some of the qualities of that third party to empower your own personality and bring new life into your relationship.

FINDING
THE CURE IN
THE LURE

WHAT TURNS YOU ON?

I f you find yourself attracted to someone else, look but don't leap. Being attracted to a third party is an intrusion on your intimacy with your partner – but there is a redeeming element here that can be used to turn this into a relationship plus. The very feature you find alluring in the third party can be used as a diagnostic tool to pinpoint changes that need to be made within yourself or your relationship. The "Cure is in the Lure Meditation" at the end of this chapter will help you make these changes.

An interesting preliminary step in this process is to identify very specifically what is magnetizing you. It will become clearer if you think of it in the following categories:

✤ physical
✤ sexual
✤ emotional
✤ intellectual
✤ spiritual

Physical Attraction: Color

Dark skin, milky white skin, blonde, brunette, redhead. Stop for a moment and think about what each of these signifies to you. Everyone has a different response. For some, dark skin is associated with passion, intrigue, strength. For others, it is unfortunately a symbol of inferiority. What makes a blonde, redhead, or brunette more or less desirable to you? Does it suggest the comfort of being at home with the familiar or perhaps the opposite – the excitement of the unknown? Jacob's story illustrates how hair color can be significant.

CASE VIGNETTE: JACOB

Jacob, a middle-aged pillar of the Jewish community, fell in love with Connie, a blonde Protestant. He was tortured by conflicting guilt and desire every time he thought of her. Using the "Cure is in the Lure Meditation" (page 158), Jacob learned his desire for Connie represented an attempt to solve several major problems. Foremost, being with someone of a different faith served as a declaration of freedom from traditions he was experiencing as suffocating. This included breaking loose from the expectation that he would devote all his life energy to being a perfect Jewish husband and father.

Physical Size

Women generally prefer taller, larger men in order to feel "protected." Men like feeling big and protective. It enables them to experience the nurturing part of themselves without their sense of masculinity being threatened. Size is also associated with physical strength. The person who feels weak physically or emotionally may be attracted to someone big in the fantasy that they will provide the strength they are missing.

Physical Energy

If you are a person with low physical energy who moves slowly, physical ebullience might be alluring. If you are easily excitable, a serene mate might be very appealing. If you have serious physical restrictions, you may need someone physically fit to help you. This can become psychologically tricky, as it did for Thomas.

CASE VIGNETTE: THOMAS

T homas was a paraplegic who had done a magnificent job of creating an active life for himself, despite his severe physical limitations. He ran a thriving business and was married to a lovely woman who respected his strengths and enjoyed taking care of him physically. They had created a good marriage, which was both sexually and emotionally fulfilling. It came to a halt when his wife, Mary, wanted to have a baby. Thomas began dreaming of other women. He started to push Mary away. He feared and resented needing her so much. Previously, he had gratefully asked for and accepted her physical help. But the responsibility of raising a child to fulfill Mary's dream of motherhood felt like a restrictive commitment that added to his physical limitations. He attempted to alleviate the fear of having to share Mary's attention by having an affair. The emotional "freedom" he envisioned eased the terror of his physical paralysis, but it led to the dissolution of his marriage.

Emotional Attraction

Is the person to whom you are attracted warm and support-ive, a practical planner, or a creative dreamer? Is that person childlike in their enthusiasm, quiet, warm, and strong in the face of adversity? Playful? A hard worker? If any of these or other emotional facets of your personality haven't been developed or aren't fulfilled in some way by your partner, obtaining them can become a driving force in your life.

When someone comes along who appears to have the nec-essary attributes to fill that void, you become emotionally attracted to them. This can extend into a physical attraction that becomes too strong to resist. The following case vignettes illustrate this process:

CASE VIGNETTE: PRISCILLA

Priscilla, a tiny, thin ball of energy, worked for a publishing company. Her husband was a romantic artist who loved her deeply. Though talented in her own right, she discounted her intelligence and assumed that men were smarter than she was. Because of her slight figure, she felt inadequate as a woman. She developed a crush on her tall, handsome boss who had a precise answer for everything. Feeling close to his power gave her a sense of security she didn't feel with her husband.

CASE VIGNETTE: ANTHONY

*A*nthony's affair was based on needs that had been buried
deeply when he was a child. He was a dapper, tense man –
short, wiry, apparently in top shape. His appearance was that of
a lightweight boxer wearing a beautifully tailored suit. He punc-
tuated his words by pounding his fist into his left hand as if that
hand had been responsible for the affair that was threatening his
family.

By extraordinary effort and perseverance, Anthony had ele-
vated himself out of an impoverished family background to
become CEO of a large chain of retail stores. Although he had
provided his wife and kids with a big house and several cars, his
family resented him for being controlling and distant. Aware of
his family's bitterness, he didn't feel at home in his own house. He
found an apparent refuge in Peggy, his attractive secretary, who
admired him and took care of him in many ways. A business trip
provided the opportunity for a brief affair that ignited passions
Anthony hadn't felt in years.

Peggy, married and the mother of two children, felt too guilty
to pursue the relationship and tearfully resigned from her job.
Anthony's wife, meanwhile, learned of the affair and threatened
divorce.

When he first came to see me, Anthony was lonely and
despondent. By using the Inner Self Meditation (see Chapter 2),
he discovered that instead of nurturing his inner self, he had
always bullied himself into achieving. He realized that he had
bullied his family in the same manner. In a later session, it
became clear to him that what he had wanted from Peggy wasn't
sex – it was nurturing. Using the same perseverance that had

brought him financial success, Anthony slowly developed the ability to be tender and caring toward himself and his family. After some initial resistance, his family began to trust his changed behavior and the healing process began. On his final visit to my office six months later, Anthony tearfully reported how wonderful it was to feel "at home" for the first time in his life.

Spiritual and Moral Attraction

You might feel uncomfortable in your relationship with someone of a different religion and background and fall for a person of your own faith who makes you feel more at home. The reverse can also be true. If you trap yourself in religious dogma with your spouse, you might seek release by pairing with someone whose religion is foreign to yours or to a person with deep spiritual values not tied to any religion.

Sharing your growing curiosity and excitement about spirituality – a force that transcends individual boundaries – promotes an exciting feeling of intimacy that can be as intense and rewarding as the best sexual intimacy. What's more, that feeling can last much longer. If you are missing this in your relationship, you may find yourself looking for it elsewhere.

CASE VIGNETTE: MARTHA

Martha left her first husband to marry Bill, who was fun and earthy. They had great sex together and were wonderful playmates for each other. Her attraction to Bill slowly waned, however, as she fell in love with Joseph, a Sunday school teacher at her church. He was kind and ethical and had a deeply spiritual and sincere love for others. Martha saw that he took great care not to hurt others and that he emanated the spiritual and moral qualities she hadn't developed in herself.

Intellectual Attraction

If you don't use your muscles, they become flabby and you feel apathetic and weak. The same is true of your brain. If you don't stimulate it by learning new things, your mind becomes blunt, passive, and listless. If you and your partner are both like this, you are liable to resent each other as intellectual couch potatoes. Instead of generating an interest in learning new things yourself, you might latch on to a third party to bring an intellectual spark to your life

SEX

"If you don't give it to me, someone else will."

The "it" word, of course, is sex. But what it stands for can be anything: pleasure, physical relief, self-esteem, a sense of femininity or masculinity, power, excitement, fun, nurturing, relief from isolation, intimacy, youthfulness, freedom, and a host of other things. Sex in our culture is used like a highly advertised credit card that can presumably get you anything. But what many people don't realize is that you have to pay dearly for it later if you don't have the currency to back it up.

And what is the back-up currency for sex? The answer is true love. When sex is an expression of love, it can convey or enhance all of the things listed above and more. Without the protective cloak of love, sex becomes more like a manipulative weapon that uses another person's body to get something instead of the expression of caring, joy, and excitement it is meant to be. Whenever sex isn't an expression of love, conflicts often arise because people feel used, manipulated, or even less than human.

Routine Sex is Destructive

Many couples have sex in the same way at the same time under the same conditions. When this is the case, sex becomes a boring routine used to relieve tension. Inevitably, one of the partners feels used and the other feels uncared for. The resulting lack of fulfillment and excitement, coupled with resentment, breeds conditions ripe for affairs.

It is our nature to take what we have for granted. Your partner becomes a "thing" – something you own that you expect to be there for you. The "thing" you want to have sex with is, of course, a living human being with fiery emotions and needs that are always changing. To have intercourse with them as if they were merely a lump of flesh provided only for your pleasure is dehumanizing – for both parties.

It is imperative to stay in touch with your emotions and those of your partner. Each variant of the sex act can be a beautiful expression of shared feelings: giving, taking, feeding, nursing, playing, expressing masculinity and femininity, strength and tenderness. How does your body want to express these things sexually? When involved in a loving exchange, there is no such thing as perversion. What you do sexually is another expression of "how many ways can I tell you I love you?" We'll return to this theme in the final chapter.

LUST BUT DON'T LEAP

I f you do start longing to have sex with someone else, look deeply within yourself to see what you really want. Don't stop at "That body really turns me on…" It's not that person's body that is turned on – it's you. Find out how you keep yourself from experiencing that same excitement with your partner. By working together, you can overcome the problem. The information in Chapter 6 can serve as a helpful starting point.

THE CURE IS IN THE LURE MEDITATION

When you touch someone with your eyes and your heart, when you are mindful of their beauty and positive attributes, it is a gift to yourself and to them. But trying to possess them, particularly if you are in a committed relationship with someone else, discounts your own potentials and causes harm to everyone else involved.

Giving up the person you are attracted to, or are having an affair with, is difficult. You might even feel as if your life isn't worth living without them. Fortunately, you don't have to give up what they represent in your life. Using the following procedures will make it easier to let go physically, and enable you to use your experience to strengthen yourself and to nurture, rather than destroy, your relationship.

The seeds of whatever it is that attracts you already lie within you. If they didn't, you wouldn't be able to appreciate those traits in someone else.

Repeating the procedures you are about to learn whenever you long for the third party will nourish those potentials within yourself and free you to bring them home to revive your relationship.

1 *Identify what it is about the third party that attracts you at this moment. What is the special characteristic they have that you want more of right now?*
2 *Imagine breathing in the essence of that quality. You might visualize it as a form of light or feel it as a warm sensation moving through your body.*
3 *Experience your body and mind as a liquid crystal being enhanced and transformed by this new form of energy. Let it move into every cell from your toes to the top of your head.*
4 *Visualize yourself using the new part of your personality in a manner that is most comfortable or enjoyable to you.*
5 *Share your newfound skill with your partner and children in an appropriate way. Keep practicing this until it becomes an automatic part of you. (This may take several months.)*
6 *In your imagination:*

a) Say goodbye to the third party

b) See them walking away forever

c) Let yourself grieve if necessary

Use the Inner Self Meditation you learned in Chapter 2 to nur-ture yourself through the pain of separation. Even if you have had no direct contact with the person, saying goodbye to a dream can be painful. If you have had extensive contact, this grief procedure may have to be repeated many times.

This six-step process will become easier each time you prac-tice it. Soon, you will be able to do it in a minute or two. Before long, it will become automatic so that you can quickly end up feeling better rather than sad when a memory of the third party pops into your mind.

CASE VIGNETTE: WILMA

Wilma was a real estate agent who spent many weekends and evenings away from home, showing houses to clients. Max, her husband, at first resented her absences openly. Then he settled into a routine of low-grade irritation and criticism. They rarely made love. As the gulf between them grew, Wilma escaped more and more often to her office and developed a crush on Jeff, a colleague.

Wilma found herself thinking of Jeff many times during the day. She kept hoping to catch a glimpse of him in the office. When *they did meet, Jeff was always warm and complimentary. She felt wonderful being around him.*

Jeff was tall and good-looking. Wilma was surprised that the quality she most longed for when she thought of Jeff wasn't sexual fulfillment – it was the feeling of total acceptance he extended to her.

Wilma learned to breathe in the spirit of self-acceptance each time she thought of Jeff. She visualized accepting her inner self unconditionally. This altered her old habit of being self-critical – a condition that had plagued her all her life. She began staying at home more often and made a point of being warm and complimentary to Max every time she thought of Jeff. Her new behavior taught her husband how to be more supportive of her. She asked Max to call attention to it whenever she criticized herself. As she experienced the warmth of her husband's support, the old sexual attraction she had felt for him early in their marriage returned.

CASE VIGNETTE: MARVIN

M*arvin loved Rose, his wife of 30 years, but was turned off by the signs of physical withering brought on by middle age. His lack of attraction to his wife led to a troublesome crush on a woman who had recently moved in next door. A 25-year-old beauty, who was also outgoing and friendly, she appealed so strongly to Marvin that he found himself hoping for a chance to see her whenever he left his house.*

But Marvin turned this attraction into a positive. Instead of giving in to his desire for the neighbor, Marvin savored breathing

in the essence of her youthful beauty and sent it out to Rose in the
form of fresh appreciation of the wonderful loving qualities she'd
always had. He did this every time he noticed wrinkles or other
signs of Rose's aging. Within a few weeks, Marvin's appreciation
of Rose's inner beauty extended to her outer appearance. He felt
more attracted to his middle-aged Rose and less turned on by the
appearance of his young neighbor. He could look at her as super-
ficially pretty, but lacking Rose's inner beauty and depth.

SUMMARY

In this chapter you learned how to avoid drowning in your desire for an affair and to use the very elements that attract you to another person as a springboard to improving your marriage or relationship.

Read on and you will discover ways to transform that person to whom you may have been tempted to be unfaithful – your husband, wife, significant other – into the soul mate you are yearning for. That is the ultimate climax.

CREATING A
SOUL MATE

WHERE IS YOUR SOUL MATE?

L isten to the silence. You may hear the faint rustle of angel wings. Here she comes – the radiance of smile, the tenderness of voice and touch, the enthusiasm of loving presence lift you beyond body to spirit as you respond in kind. You are fully alive, but beyond life. This moment with your beloved has no beginning and no end. You are soul mates, safe in God's cocoon, a place that has no barriers.

You don't have to drown in loneliness and longing. You don't have to put an ad in the paper or search for a special connection everywhere you go. The rustle of angel wings surrounds you right where you are. Soul mates are everywhere, hidden in earthbound disguises.

Everything we have talked about up to now was preparation for opening up to the soul mate you wake up with every day. Discovering your life partner as a soul mate is the ultimate fruition of the art of intimacy. As with every art, it gets better with practice.

You create a soul mate when you add the power of spiritual love to an intimate relationship – where love reigns supreme. Here are some guidelines that have heavenly payoffs. Think of these guidelines as statements of intent that are pleasurable to carry out as expressions of caring. When you slip up on any of these, congratulate yourself on being aware of the lapse and enjoy recommitting yourself to a love that keeps blossoming.

Divine Thought

When you think of your lover, surround each thought with joyful appreciation for the miracle of their presence on earth. Each thought we have has deep roots in the past. Embracing the thought with love strengthens the roots of affection from the past in the unconscious mind and predisposes you toward loving association in the present and future. As you touch the thought with mindful awareness and let it go, it is replaced by another thought that has deeper, more spiritual wisdom.

Defusing Noxious Thoughts

It is important to become aware of any concept or generalization you have made about your partner that is detrimental to love, and replace it with compassion and understanding. That doesn't mean you have to agree with or approve of everything your partner says or does. It does mean, however, that any changes you would like them to make will be addressed with caring understanding. In this way the two of you become a united front inviting change that is in the loving best interests of you both.

For example, your mate may tend to be disorderly and leave their belongings all over the house. You might think to yourself, "What a pig!" This is a generalization that obstructs loving feelings and disturbs you, even if it is not verbalized. If expressed openly, it invites defensiveness and anger in return. Over a period of time, you may have watered so many seeds of disdain in your unconscious mind that what grows from them may eventually crowd out the seeds of love. The appellation for your partner in this scenario of your conscious mind may change from "darling" to "pig."

How to Turn a Pig into a Prince

How do you turn a pig into a prince? Basically, you do it the same way the mythical princess in the story books did it when she turned a frog into a prince with a kiss. Everyone has different standards for tidiness. Here's a way to dealing internally with disorder. You can use this format to deal with any other qualities in your partner, as well.

1   Make a list of all the things about your partner that you love. Feel gratefulness for each one. Verbalize your appreciation frequently.
2   Imagine that everything in your home was in perfect order – but your mate is no longer with you. Is your love for orderliness greater than your love for your mate? If so, check your value system. Which one is closer to God – orderliness or a loving relationship?

It is true that it is much easier to feel at peace and accomplish things in an orderly environment than it is when things are messy around you. There is no need to give up that desire, but remember that happiness does not come from changing your environment. You can be content with yourself in this moment no matter what is going on around you.

How to Ask for What You Want
Without being critical, tell your partner how important this issue is for you. Using caring words, ask for their help.

What if Your Partner Doesn't Change?
Being disorderly can be a deep-seated habit based upon many factors that we don't have time to discuss here. But note that if your partner seems unable to change, perhaps you could negotiate having a space of your own where they agree not to intrude. Enjoy keeping your private space as neat as you wish.

Open Your Heart
Blow a kiss at your lover's mess whenever you notice it. You are sweetening the pot instead of poisoning the well. Your acceptance may in fact give your loved one the strength to tackle what for them is a mountainous task.

Divine Speech

Everything we have said about thoughts applies tenfold to speech. Every word you say to your lover can radiate beauty, harmony, and love to them and between you both. **An angry word is like a hand grenade thrown into the temple of love.** If you recognize yourself feeling angry, congratulate yourself for being aware of it and not expressing it. But anger is not to be suppressed; it serves as a bookmark that signals a need for change. Reviewing Chapter 10 will help you transform anger into compassion and understanding.

Truthfulness

It goes without saying that there can be no love and trust without truthfulness. Lies have the same destructive energy as rage. If you have done something your partner may not approve of, it is far better to discuss it openly than to hide it.

Divine Hearing

We are always involved in some preoccupying thought or action. It requires generosity of spirit to stop and give the love of your life the full attention they need when they speak to you. Let your mind be like a quiet pond that reflects whatever your partner is saying. You are not rehearsing a response or reacting judgmentally. You are listening with an open heart. A response that you are totally there listening in a warm and caring manner validates your partner's existence and, in turn, also validates your own caring nature.

Divine Seeing

Each time you see your lover is an opportunity to silently experience the wonder that, out of all the people in the world, this person has chosen you for his or her devotion. Let that loving feeling turn into excitement at their presence. Feel the energy coursing through your body. Let that positive spirit erase any judgmental thoughts you may have about them.

Divine Touch

Let the energy of caring and love course through your body. Don't hesitate to allow your body to express it with any kind of loving touch that feels appropriate. Chapter 8 explains ways in which you can use sensual feelings that may arise to enhance love and turn love into sexy soul food.

Sharing Enthusiasm

Do you remember the excitement you felt when a child you love took that very first step? The burst of enthusiasm came from your heart. It is interesting to note that the word "enthusiasm" derives from the Greek "being in God." Celebrating your partner's efforts and achievements with enthusiasm is God-like endorsement that brings lightness into the relationship. It is equally important to share that same enthusiasm about yourself. Sharing enthusiasm with each other is the nirvana of love.

Patience

Impatience is the opposite of love. You become irritated by your partner's failure to understand you or to act quickly. Tapping your fingers impatiently or letting out exasperated sighs can be perceived as a painful assault. The way to become patient is to practice it. Become aware of the tension in your body that is signaling annoyance. Take a deep breath, relax as you exhale the tension, and welcome tender, supportive feelings as you breathe in again.

Compassion

When your beloved is expressing painful feelings or responding fearfully to some traumatic experience, put yourself in
their place so you can experience some of the pain they are
going through. Move into the loving part of yourself by
recalling a time when you felt nurturing. Watch your breath.
Imagine breathing in the painful emotions that your partner
is expressing, opening the space around your heart to them.
As you breathe out, send them love. Hold them as you do
this. If they don't want to be held, do it from a distance.
Don't brush them off with platitudes or by simply telling
them things will be okay, or even by giving advice. Simply
stay there patiently accepting their pain and send them loving energy, as long as it takes to help them achieve a feeling
of being peaceful.

No Avoidance

Our tendency is to avoid pain, anger, grief, sadness, or fear
in our lovers and in ourselves. We would like such feelings
to simply go away. It is important, however, to be aware of
the physical sensations you have when these emotions are
being expressed, either by yourself or your lover. Watch
your breath and become more and more mindful of the
nature of these emotions and your reaction to them. It is
interesting that men in particular often avoid any emotion
that might label them as weak. This is indicated by shallow
breathing and muscle tension. To counteract this, breathe
deeply into the area that is tense. It will help break the dam

of tension and let the emotions flow. Going through pain together with loving acceptance opens up your heart and your arms to each other.

No Attachment

When we enjoy someone's company and are used to their caring presence, we tend to become attached to them. Realize that you are the one having the good feelings. It is wonderful to have your lover there as a catalyst, but don't become deluded by the idea that they must be attached to you for you to feel good. This leads to a need to control them instead of caring for them.

No Control

We are so used to controlling ourselves that it becomes second nature to want to control those we are closest to. The first three chapters of this book described how we put uncaring controls over ourselves rather than inspiring ourselves to live a life that is free and safe at the same time. Anytime you feel tension when you are with your partner, stop and notice if there is something you are trying to control in them. Unsolicited advice discounts your partner's intelligence. Your intentions may be good, but if your partner reacts with irritation or distance to some suggestion you make, the chances are you are being controlling. My wife becomes annoyed with me whenever I slip and tell her what she should be doing. To counteract this trait, take a deep breath, relax as you exhale, and feel admiration for your partner as an independent, free human being. When the issue is something that affects you both – such as money or sex – work out a compromise that honors both of you.

A MEDITATION THAT TRANSFORMS YOUR EARTH MATE INTO A SOUL MATE

Priming Your Heart Pump. *Shift your focus from the thoughts circling through your head to those in your heart. Breathe in and out of your heart as if it were your lungs. As you breathe in, remember all the things you love about your earth mate and the first time you met them. Each time you do this, open your heart to any quality they have that is precious to you. As you breathe out, send that quality back to them.*

Soul Mate Talk. *Let your mind be an open pond, effortlessly mirroring each thought, as if your thoughts were stones rippling the waters of the pond. Watch each thought and its ripples and let them go. Whenever your mind wanders, gently refocus it on a loving thought emanating from your heart. You will notice that your thoughts become less frequent and diminish in emotional intensity. Touching each thought with loving awareness becomes a magic wand. Out of the silence of the disappearing thought so touched emerges a new thought cloaked in universal wisdom and love. This is a message you can share directly with your soul mate.*

THE ULTIMATE IN INTIMACY

The mystery and excitement of a budding romance between you and your life partner is here for you right now. Here we are talking about the ultimate in intimacy.

Buddha made a startling observation that is as true today as it was millennia ago when he discovered it – all of us are in a constant emerging into a new self. We are never the same from moment to moment. How we are re-created depends upon an infinite number of causes and conditions that reflect a universe constantly in flux. He referred to that state as "dependent co-arising." This means that everything in the universe, including you and your mate, is interdependent and effecting modifications in us all of the time. It's like the gumballs in a machine – each one influences all of the others and has an effect on which one will pop out of the machine.

Bear with me: What you are about to read is tremendously important in our journey to intimacy – and it's mind-boggling. Since we are always changing, any label we put on each other is based on our imagination, not on reality. If I label my wife as wonderful or dreadful, that is a handle I put on her so that my mind has something to grab on to. But it is a statement I dreamed up that doesn't reflect the reality of her ever-changing self. The label – whether positive or negative – actually distances me from her true self.

Naturally, I tend to cling to the positive label and back away from the negative. But the answer for me, to be truly intimate with her, is to embrace her with love and compassion – the essence of her as a cherished, emerging spirit whom I and everything else in the universe is influencing.

THE ROMANCE OF SOUL MATES
(A MEDITATION)

Hold hands
Breathe together as one
Lose yourself in your lover's gaze
Feel the tingle of luminous energy coursing through you
Mind and body dissolve in God's embrace
Two oceans of love
Touching
Never the same
A romance of souls together that has no end.

POSTSCRIPT

Writing this book has been a beautiful gift to myself. As it was coming to fruition, I was going through an especially difficult time in my marriage. This book gave me a wonderful opportunity to test first-hand most of the concepts that have been successfully employed in my psychiatric practice.

With a lump in my throat (okay, I just breathed in the lump and turned it into tears of gratefulness), I feel bathed in a joyful warmth and security that embraces generations of teachers, my wife, and you, dear reader. May we never give up developing a loving intimacy with each other and all of God's creation.

RECOMMENDED READING

Reb Anderson, *Zen's Chinese Heritage: The Masters and Their Teachings* (Wisdom Publications, 2000)

Mary McClure Goulding and Robert L. Goulding, *Changing Lives Through Redecision Therapy* (Grove Press, 1997)

— *Not to Worry! How to Free Yourself from Unnecessary Anxiety and Channel Your Worries into Positive Action* (William Morrow, 1989)

Robert L. Goulding and Mary McClure Goulding, *The Power is in the Patient: A TA/Gestalt Approach to Psychotherapy* (Trans Pub, 1978)

Thich Nhat Hanh, *Peace is Every Step: The Path of Mindfulness in Everyday Life* (Bantam, 1992)

—*The Art of Mindful Living: How to Bring Love, Compassion and Inner Peace Into Your Daily Life* (audio CD, Sounds True, 2000)

—*Breathe! You Are Alive: Sutra on the Full Awareness of Breathing* (Parallax Press, 1996)

—*Teachings on Love* (Parallax Press, 1998)

Also by Arthur Samuels, M.D.

THE ART OF SAYING GOODBYE

How to Survive the Loss of a Love

Grief can be a measure of how well you have lived and how deeply you have loved. *The Art of Saying Goodbye* is a powerful statement of comfort and hope that will:

❖ Show you how to love yourself through the excruciating pain of losing a loved one
❖ Teach you how to transform the essence of your loss into a powerful part of your personality
❖ Enable you to savour the preciousness of this moment, the only moment you can be truly alive

If you bring your body and experience to read this book, it will become a source of tremendous help. Thich Nhat Hanh

A compelling, readable book that brings a wealth of wisdom and practical insights for anyone who will ever have to deal with grief – in other words, every one of us. Rabbi Earl A. Grollman

Make
www.thorsonselement.com
your online sanctuary

www.thorsonselement.com

thorsons
element